PRAISE FOR *TAKE CHARGE OF YOUR NURSING CAREER*, SECOND EDITION

"Lois Marshall and her contributors have done it again! The second edition of Take Charge of Your Nursing Career *reminds all nurses how essential intentional career planning is, whether it is developing, managing, or expanding one's career. This incredible resource is well-written, relevant, timely, and important and offers numerous practical tips, strategies, and tools all nurses can use on their career journey."*

–Carol Huston, DPA, MSN, FAAN
Professor Emerita, School of Nursing, Trinity Hall
California State University, Chico

"A practical approach for developing self-as-nurse written by leaders in the profession. The personal exemplars and thoughtful questions for self-discovery begin the reflective process necessary to be successful from your first job to taking on new positions in academia, administration, advanced practice, entrepreneurship, policy, and/or research. This inspirational guide covers additional content of mentorship, advocacy, and social media to enhance your evolving nursing identity. A must-read and resource for every nurse's library."

–Colleen Maykut, DNP, RN
Professor, Faculty of Nursing, Department of Health Systems & Sustainability,
MacEwan University
Fellow Canadian Academy of Nursing (FCAN) Inaugural Class 2020
Pronouns: She/Her/Hers

"Lois Marshall is a fierce advocate, mentor, and friend to nurses around the world. As such, she has written a must-read for those looking to start, change, or advance their nursing careers. I have and will always refer my new graduate nursing students to Lois Marshall for the right way to begin their nursing journey."

–Jessica Marcus, DNP, RN, WHNP-BC
Clinical Assistant Professor, School of Nursing
Byrdi--- Lewis College of Nursing & Health Professions
Georgia State University

T0281780

"*Brilliant—Dr. Marshall's book guides nurses with steps to taking their nursing career to the next level. She takes you on a dynamic journey of identifying your nursing identity and how to market it in the workforce. Dr. Marshall is an exceptional nurse educator and a masterful writer who, through this book, reveals several techniques to catapult one's nursing career. This comprehensive, in-depth text was long overdue.*"

–Donna Carrazzone, DNP, FNP-C, RN, AHN-BC
Assistant Professor, Caldwell University

"*The renowned author and contributors provide sage advice about managing your nursing career through all stages. From defining your nursing identity to marketing yourself, the book offers guidance for multiple situations. Professional development through continuing education and mentorship demonstrates routes to ongoing advancement. Tips and notes, embedded in each chapter, provide salient, practical advice. Vignettes of nurses from different phases of their careers describe personal, meaningful experiences related to the focus of each chapter.*"

–Mary Lou Bond, PhD, RN, CNE, ANEF, FAAN
Professor Emerita, The University of Texas at Arlington,
College of Nursing and Health Innovation
Adjunct Faculty, Texas Christian University, College of Nursing and Health Sciences

"*Dr. Lois Marshall is one of the world's foremost experts on career development in the nursing profession, and she has already helped thousands of nurses navigate their nursing journey over the course of her career—including me. She is a treasure to the profession, and her book provides much more insight than typical career advice. It is an indispensable resource for nurses at any stage of their career.*"

–Kevin Lillis, MPH, BSN, RN, CNRN
Unit Charge Nurse, Neurosurgical ICU
Emory University Hospital

"A practical and easy-to-read book for nurses who would like to expand their professional pathways. Readers can greatly benefit from the conversational writing style, well-pitched chapters, small boxes of notes and tips, and reflective questions, as well as resources and examples. And of course, readers can easily find themselves in short vignettes shared by nurses who have been-there-done-that with those same self-doubts or struggles like you and me at some stage in our careers."

–Van N. B. Nguyen, PhD, MN, BN
Nurse Researcher
Melbourne, Australia

"Dr. Marshall authored the book Take Charge of Your Nursing Career to encourage nurses to advocate for their careers and make informed decisions. This book is easy to read and constantly engages the reader in the endless opportunities available in the nursing profession. The chapters will empower readers to navigate through the different facets of their careers and drive their professional journey. Novice and experienced nurses will genuinely enjoy the valuable gems shared in each chapter."

–LaToya Lewis, Ed.D-CI, MSN, RN
Assistant Professor of Clinical, University of Miami School of
Nursing and Health Studies
Associate Editor, ABNFJ

"I love that this book is created as a workbook for nurses at every level to be self-directed and take control of their career and future. More than ever, nurses need a marketing plan that promotes their professional identity, career objectives, and resiliency. Dr. Marshall is a champion of career resilience dedicated to continuous learning and promoting professional nursing practice autonomy, self-direction, and full scope of practice. Create your career vision plan at your pace."

–Carole Kulik, DNP, RN, ACNP-BC, HCIC
Assistant Professor, San Francisco State University
CNO, Clinical Executives

"As you embark on your nursing career or even are transitioning to a new stage, there are endless pathways and opportunities for growth and advancement in the nursing profession. Take Charge of Your Nursing Career *gives you the resources, skills, and information you need to champion your own way through an exciting professional pathway as you assess the risks and benefits of your next career decision. Dr. Marshall and her colleagues give you the tools to explore the variety of options at your fingertips, empowering you to open and close all the right doors. Read this book today and confidently choose your nursing path."*

–Trisha Mims, MSN, MBA, RN, HCM
Director of Program and Education
National Student Nurses' Association

"I had the good fortune to be professionally mentored by Dr. Lois Marshall. Her confidence and passionate support changed my career trajectory and influenced where I am today. That passion, support, and confidence shines through in her book, and I hope it influences others the way it has me. I hope one day I can make just as big of an impact in the world of nursing as Dr. Marshall has!"

–Kathryn C. Hansen, BSN, RN
Nurse, Mother/Baby Department
Northwestern Medicine Prentice Women's Hospital

TAKE CHARGE

OF YOUR

NURSING
CAREER

SECOND EDITION

LOIS SARAH MARSHALL, PHD, MN, RN

Sigma
GLOBAL NURSING
EXCELLENCE

Copyright © 2022 by Sigma Theta Tau International Honor Society of Nursing

All rights reserved. This book is protected by copyright. No part of it may be reproduced, stored in a retrieval system, or transmitted in any form or by any means, electronic, mechanical, photocopying, recording, or otherwise, without written permission from the publisher. Any trademarks, service marks, design rights, or similar rights that are mentioned, used, or cited in this book are the property of their respective owners. Their use here does not imply that you may use them for a similar or any other purpose.

This book is not intended to be a substitute for the medical advice of a licensed medical professional. The author and publisher have made every effort to ensure the accuracy of the information contained within at the time of its publication and shall have no liability or responsibility to any person or entity regarding any loss or damage incurred, or alleged to have incurred, directly or indirectly, by the information contained in this book. The author and publisher make no warranties, express or implied, with respect to its content, and no warranties may be created or extended by sales representatives or written sales materials. The author and publisher have no responsibility for the consistency or accuracy of URLs and content of third-party websites referenced in this book.

Sigma Theta Tau International Honor Society of Nursing (Sigma) is a nonprofit organization whose mission is developing nurse leaders anywhere to improve healthcare everywhere. Founded in 1922, Sigma has more than 135,000 active members in over 100 countries and territories. Members include practicing nurses, instructors, researchers, policymakers, entrepreneurs, and others. Sigma's more than 540 chapters are located at more than 700 institutions of higher education throughout Armenia, Australia, Botswana, Brazil, Canada, Colombia, Croatia, England, Eswatini, Ghana, Hong Kong, Ireland, Israel, Italy, Jamaica, Japan, Jordan, Kenya, Lebanon, Malawi, Mexico, the Netherlands, Nigeria, Pakistan, Philippines, Portugal, Puerto Rico, Scotland, Singapore, South Africa, South Korea, Sweden, Taiwan, Tanzania, Thailand, the United States, and Wales. Learn more at www.sigmanursing.org.

Sigma Theta Tau International
550 West North Street
Indianapolis, IN, USA 46202

To request a review copy for course adoption, order additional books, buy in bulk, or purchase for corporate use, contact Sigma Marketplace at 888.654.4968 (US/Canada toll-free), +1.317.687.2256 (International), or solutions@sigmamarketplace.org.

To request author information, or for speaker or other media requests, contact Sigma Marketing at 888.634.7575 (US/Canada toll-free) or +1.317.634.8171 (International).

ISBN: 9781646480005
EPUB ISBN: 9781646480074
PDF ISBN: 9781646480067
MOBI ISBN: 9781646480081

Library of Congress Cataloging-in-Publication data

Names: Marshall, Lois, 1956- author.

Title: Take charge of your nursing career / Lois Sarah Marshall, PhD, MN, RN.

Description: Second edition. | Indianapolis, IN : Sigma Theta Tau International, [2022] | Includes bibliographical references and index. | Summary: "A career is a fluid process, not stagnant or simply a job. It is a process that must be nurtured--constantly grown and managed. Today, nursing professionals across the globe and at each stage in their career consistently ask how to navigate, grow, and expand their careers; change their career trajectories; and develop, hone, and promote their nursing identities. Nurses are focused on career-development and management areas that are far beyond writing a resumé or curriculum vitae. They are looking for career resources that apply to the many roles and challenges they face at all points and phases of their career. This book provides just that. Take Charge of Your Nursing Career, Second Edition, provides nurses with a unique and distinct perspective to develop and manage their careers from beginning to end. With timely and relevant topics, strategies, tips, and examples, author Lois Sarah Marshall helps nurses define their personal career trajectory no matter what point they are in their journey"-- Provided by publisher.

Identifiers: LCCN 2021042355 (print) | LCCN 2021042356 (ebook) | ISBN
   9781646480005 (paperback) | ISBN 9781646480074 (epub) | ISBN
   9781646480067 (pdf) | ISBN 9781646480081 (mobi)
Subjects: LCSH: Nursing--Vocational guidance. | Career development.
Classification: LCC RT82 .M224 2022 (print) | LCC RT82 (ebook) | DDC
   610.7306/9--dc23
LC record available at https://lccn.loc.gov/2021042355
LC ebook record available at https://lccn.loc.gov/2021042356

First Printing, 2021

Publisher: Dustin Sullivan
Acquisitions Editor: Emily Hatch
Development Editor: Kate Shoup
Cover Designer: Rebecca Batchelor
Interior Design/Page Layout: Rebecca Batchelor

Managing Editor: Carla Hall
Publications Specialist: Todd Lothery
Copy Editor: Todd Lothery
Proofreader: Erin Geile
Indexer: Larry Sweazy

DEDICATION

This book is dedicated to the women who make up my "rings of power." I wear their rings on a necklace that empowers me and gives me the confidence to be my authentic self. The rings represent my great grandmother Sarah, my grandmother Doris, my mother Ada, and my daughter Lauren. In their own ways, throughout my life and career, each one has affected and influenced me, pushed me, given me strength, and shown me the way. When I need them and their power, I hold onto my necklace and remind myself that they are always with me. Their belief in me gives me the drive to always move forward. This book is a culmination of what they have taught me: to never forget where I came from and what I have learned that I can then impart to others, to use my voice to pay it forward, to always be my unique and true self, and most importantly, that my nursing career was always where I was meant to make my unique difference.

ACKNOWLEDGMENTS

First and foremost, I wish to express my sincere gratitude to the numerous professional nurses who gave—and continue to give—me the opportunity to mentor them along their career paths, from new graduates though retirement and even beyond. They have inspired me, and it is because of them and their career questions and inquiries, in person and virtually, that I was excited to continue to write about one of my passions: career development and management for all nurses.

My family, from here and from above, always remind(ed) me that anything is possible, and that I can do whatever I set my mind to on my career journey, despite obstacles and unexpected turns and twists. My parents left with me their work ethic and their principles to never forget where I came from and to always give back using my authentic and unique voice. I hope they know I do that every day.

To the mentors throughout my career, beginning with my mother, a diploma nursing school graduate in the 1950s, my thanks do not seem enough. My mentors have taught me so much and continue to do so anytime I email them, call them, or run into them at a conference or meeting. They never hesitate to answer my questions, give me a pep talk, remind me of what I offer as a nursing professional, and guide me when I need direction. They are remarkable women who give of themselves constantly. I hope each of them knows what they mean to me and my career journey.

To the four contributors who shared their expertise in this book, there are no words to express my gratitude. Each one of them has a more than busy career and took time to share their knowledge and wisdom to empower nurses on their career journeys. Dr. Sarah E. Gray, Dr. Tina Ferrell, Dr. Matthew Howard, and Samantha Martin are excellent examples of how to navigate one's career path with excitement and curiosity, to keep seeking answers, and to maintain a desire to give back to others on their own journeys.

To my daughter Lauren, who also works as my research and editorial assistant, I cannot express my love sufficiently in words. You always believe in me and my work. You understand how much my career—and as an extension of that, this book—means to me. You know when to leave me to myself and when to jump in to help, especially with my other work. Knowing that you support me in all my endeavors is a gift that keeps on giving.

I am lucky to have a group of friends and colleagues whom I get to work with as a Sigma volunteer every day on numerous projects, including all things Sigma Career Center. Dr. Matt Howard, Samantha Martin, and Dr. Carole Kulik are my circle. We are a team. We support each other, work with each other, learn from each other, push each other to be our best, and are always there for each other. During the book-writing process, they have been my support and my eyes and ears for all things career related. There is nothing we cannot accomplish together. Because of their constant presence and support, I am who I am and get to do what I love to do.

To Emily Hatch, the acquisitions editor for Sigma Theta Tau International Honor Society of Nursing (Sigma), there is no one like you. You never saw me as just an author, but as a colleague and friend. Your support, even when not about the book, has meant so much to me. So, for putting up with my meltdowns, my excitement, my questions, my emails, and my texts, thank you for simply being you.

To every other person at Sigma who I have the privilege to interact with and collaborate with in all my volunteer work with them, thank you will never be enough. Some of you have been colleagues and friends for more years than we can count; others of you are newer colleagues and friends, but just as important to me. Through every experience in person, across the globe, virtually, or by phone, I always feel supported, and I hope you know that my support for you is unwavering as well. Writing this book and everything I do with and for Sigma is a constant reminder of how lucky I am in my career to know you all.

And far from last in my world, to Dinorah Hampton, the best cheer-leader and my rock when I needed one. There are some friends who are just meant to be. No matter what time of the day or how many times in a day, she was always there during this book process. She gave me en-couragement via text or direct messages, on videos, and during weekend calls where she listened without hesitation. She is the guardian angel of this book.

ABOUT THE AUTHOR

LOIS SARAH MARSHALL, PHD, MN, RN

Lois S. Marshall has been a nurse and nurse educator for 43 years. She continues to have a diverse and consistently evolving professional nursing career. Her career journey has taken her from full-time academics to broad-based consultation, where she has taken on challenges, embraced the many opportunities afforded to her, and grown her expertise in a wide array of areas.

The "guiding post" of many of these opportunities has been centered on the theme of career. Marshall has enhanced her work in all the facets of her own career, while at the same time mentoring others to develop, promote, challenge, and empower themselves as they navigate their own career trajectories. She has been at the forefront of nursing career development and management and all their various components over the last 10 years in her roles as lead advisor for the Sigma Career Center since 2013. Marshall has also been the coordinator of the Career Development Center for the National Student Nurses' Association since 2012.

Marshall received her BSN from the University of Miami, Florida, USA; an MN from Emory University, Atlanta, Georgia, USA; and a PhD from the University of Miami, with a focus on higher education, curriculum design, and outcomes assessment. From 1980 to 2004, Marshall held a variety of faculty and administration positions while at the University of Miami School of Nursing. She received numerous teaching awards throughout her career. In 2004, she was selected a Helene Fuld Fellow by the American Association of Colleges of Nursing. In 2019, she was honored to receive the Florida Nurses Association Mentor/Role Model ICON Award for her contributions to the nursing profession.

Marshall's research expertise is related to test-taking strategies, outcomes assessment, and evaluation related to the NCLEX-RN examination. She has been preparing nursing graduates with her own course for

40 years, locally, nationally, and internationally. Since the pandemic, Marshall has offered all her tutoring, reviews, and expertise free of charge for any nursing graduate to "pay it forward," empowering them to achieve their first nursing career success. Her current research projects relate to career development and management in the broadest sense, including some of the specific areas addressed in this book, such as mentorship.

Marshall presents statewide, nationally, and internationally on topics ranging from career advancement and related subjects, the promotion of evidence-based nursing and research, the development of abstracts for presentations and grant applications, mentorship, and leadership. She mentors Sigma members and nonmembers in exploring and articulating their career identity, advancing their careers along their chosen path(s), and achieving their career goals. She also publishes on these same topics.

Marshall has been the principal and owner of LSM Educational Consulting since 2004. Her consultative services include but are not limited to career development, management, and advancement; mentorship; NCLEX-RN/PN and test-taking preparation for individuals and groups of students, nationally and internationally, within or outside of schools and colleges of nursing; faculty development related to instruction; curriculum design and implementation; curriculum and program evaluation; evidence-based nursing practice; abstract development; small grant writing and research development; scholarly writing development; and project management.

Marshall has been the clinical editor for Elsevier's *ClinicalKey for Nursing, Evidence-Based Nursing Monographs* for 14 years. The research-based monographs are designed for bedside nurses, wherever that care is administered. These monographs have the unique feature of providing a synopsis of each of the most recent and relevant nursing and other research studies, as well as evidence-based nursing recommendations based on these synopses and current practice. The research monographs are a complete document for the nurse to provide them the information and evidence at the point of care.

Marshall is the research column editor for the *Journal of Radiology Nursing*, where she writes a quarterly column. Marshall is also the chair of the Research Special Interest Group for the Florida Nurse's Association. This committee is responsible for the coordination of the annual Research and Evidence-Based Nursing Conference.

CONTRIBUTING AUTHORS

Sarah E. Gray, DNP, RN, CEN, FAEN, is a creative visionary whose mission is to equip and empower others. She discovered her passion for service and transformational leadership during her 15 years in emergency and occupational medicine. She served as social media chair, among other roles, for the Indiana Emergency Nurses Association for six years. She is a fellow in the Academy of Emergency Nursing. Gray is currently the director of educational resources, global initiatives, and the marketplace for Sigma Theta Tau International Honor Society of Nursing (Sigma). She develops continuing education programs, domestic and international events, and opportunities for the global nursing community. In this role, she also oversees Sigma's consultative status and programming with the United Nations (UN). Gray is a presenter, author, and coach on practical solutions, innovations, and inspirational topics, specializing in professional branding and leadership. She recognizes the power of professional branding within her own professional network and endeavors. She is now sought out to share her insights on using social media and networking to cultivate current and future potential in individuals.

Christina Ferrell, PhD, RN, NEA-BC, has been a nurse for 26 years with 19 years in nursing leadership roles. Her ambition to lead and mentor has been fulfilled in roles ranging from charge nurse to nurse manager, nursing director, director of clinical excellence, director of hospital education, and Magnet program coordinator. Her current role as an assistant nursing professor and director of the RN to MSN program at the University of Mississippi Medical Center's School of Nursing continues to afford her the opportunity to support the professional growth of nurses. Her impact has been acknowledged through induction into the Norman C. Nelson Order of Teaching Excellence, University Hospitals' Leadership Excellence Award, Mississippi Nurses Association Non-traditional Nurse of the Year Award, University of Mississippi School of Nursing Distinguished Alumni of the Decade, and the Mississippi Hospital Association's Nurse Executive of the Year. Ferrell's experiences led her to a quest to understand the concept of nursing professional identity and its development over the continuum of one's career. Her PhD dissertation research focused on understanding the nursing professional identity of senior nurse leaders. Ferrell now collaborates with nurses from around the globe who share her interest in further understanding professional identity in nursing.

Matthew S. Howard, DNP, RN, CEN, TCRN, CPEN, CPN, is currently the Director of Scholarship and Leadership Resources at Sigma Theta Tau International Honor Society of Nursing (Sigma). While also serving as faculty at Northern Kentucky University, Howard works as a staff nurse in the emergency department at Eskenazi Health in Indianapolis, Indiana, USA. His nursing career has taken him from stretcher-side nursing to academia and back. His clinical background includes EMS, emergency department nursing, flight nursing, and trauma nursing, with several leadership positions. Howard serves on several local, national, and international councils and nursing associations, including the Emergency Nurses Association (ENA), the International Network for Doctoral Education in Nursing (INDEN), and Sigma, and as an advisory member to the National Nursing Education Research Network.

Samantha Martin, BA, is an experienced career program specialist with more than five years of experience working with Sigma Theta Tau International Honor Society of Nursing (Sigma). She has supported the development of the Sigma mentorship and coaching program, the Sigma mentoring cohort, and numerous other career-support programs offered through Sigma for its membership. Although she does not hold a nursing degree, she does place a strong value on evidence-based program development and has a calling to work with professional nurses to help them reach their career goals.

FREE BOOK RESOURCES

PDF versions of all the cover letters, resumés, and curriculum vitae, as well as a sample chapter, can be found online from the Sigma Repository. Visit this book's page by following the link or the QR code below.

http://hdl.handle.net/10755/21950

TABLE OF CONTENTS

About the Author xii

Foreword. xxi

Preface. xxiii

Introduction. xxv

1 THE ART AND SCIENCE OF
MARKETING YOURSELF 1

The Why of Marketing 2

Where Do I Begin?. 2

General Thoughts on Resumés and CVs 4

The Components of a Resumé. 9

Building a Curriculum Vitae 19

Introducing Yourself in a Cover Letter. 21

The Interview: It Goes Both Ways 22

2 YOUR CAREER REPOSITORY:
THE PORTFOLIO. 31

Why a Career Portfolio? 32

Your Portfolio "File Cabinet": The Components
of a Portfolio. 34

Time to Start the Process 54

References 55

3 YOUR NURSING IDENTITY 57

What Is Nursing Identity? 58

Reflecting on Your Nursing Journey 61

Defining Your Nursing Identity 62

References 66

4 EDUCATIONAL ADVANCEMENT: GAINING NEW EXPERTISE 67

Know Thyself: Deciding if Further Education Is
Right for You. 68
You've Decided . . . Now What? 70
Closing Thoughts. 86
References 87

5 PROFESSIONAL DEVELOPMENT AND CONTINUING EDUCATION: ROLE EXPANSION 89

Additional Avenues of Career Advancement 91
Where Should You Begin? 92
Finding Courses, Programs, and Academies. 93
Attending Conferences. 95
Certification and Credentialing 97
Conclusion 99

6 THE VALUE OF MENTORSHIP: A TWO-WAY PROCESS TO PAY IT FORWARD 101

Mentorship Defined. 104
The Basics: Roles, Responsibilities, Process 105
What Do You Gain from Mentorship? 108
Is Being a Mentor Right for Me? 110
Finding a Mentor. 111
Building Your Mentorship Plan 113
Techniques to Promote Successful Mentorship. 115
Potential Roadblocks to Mentorship Success. 116
Building a Mentorship Network 118
Global Mentorship 118
Some Final Words of Advice 121

7 CAREER DEVELOPMENT AND MANAGEMENT FOR INTERNATIONAL NURSES 123

Some Background 124

Cultural Impact on Career Development and
  Management 125

Relocating to North America.................. 126

Seeking a Post-Doctoral Fellowship or Other
  Education in North America 127

Relocation Across the Globe 128

Some Final Recommendations................. 132

8 USING SOCIAL MEDIA TO DEVELOP, AUGMENT, AND PROPEL YOUR CAREER.........135

Leveraging Social Media 136

Risks of Social Media 137

Benefits of Social Media...................... 139

Identifying Your Brand 141

Practical Tips to Leverage Your Social Media
  Presence for Professional Development 148

Conclusion 151

References................................. 152

9 EXPANDING YOUR REACH: USING YOUR VOICE 153

The Importance of Using Your Voice............. 154

Using Your Voice: Dissemination................ 155

Using Your Voice for Advocacy Through the Media ... 158

Using Your Voice in Professional Organizations 160

Using Your Voice as a Political Advocate......... 161

Using Your Voice to Network 162

Final Thoughts 164

References................................. 165

10 ENTREPRENEURSHIP FOR THE
    PROFESSIONAL NURSE........ 167
    Taking on New Challenges 168
    Opportunities for Nurse Entrepreneurs: A Potential
      Fit for Everyone........................... 170
    Getting Started............................. 175
    Important Considerations 178

11 WORK-LIFE BALANCE ISSUES:
    MANAGING PERSONAL AND
    PROFESSIONAL TIME.......... 187
    Work-Life Balance: The Dilemma 188
    Work-Life Balance: Our Reality of Little to None ... 189
    The Current Environment 190
    Tips and Strategies to Achieve Work-Life Balance ... 191
    Parting Personal Words 194

A   EXAMPLES OF NEW AND
    EXPERIENCED NURSE RESUMÉS ..195

B   CURRICULUM VITAE 201

C   EXAMPLE OF BLANK CV 223

D   SAMPLE COVER LETTERS 225

E   PERSONAL PHILOSOPHY
    EXAMPLE: PHILOSOPHY OF
    TEACHING 229

F   FORMAT FOR DEVELOPING
    YOUR NURSING CAREER
    IDENTITY 233

G   MENTORING AGREEMENT...... 235

    INDEX 237

FOREWORD

Reading the introduction to *Take Charge of Your Nursing Career* caused me to reflect on my own career trajectory. Books like this with relevant, practical content and strategies for career planning were not available in 1970 when I graduated. Although I have had a successful and varied career, including positions as a clinical pediatric nurse, faculty member, academic administrator, and CEO, retired, of Sigma Theta Tau International, there were challenges, disappointments, and detours along the way. The material in this book would have assisted me greatly across my journey.

Subjects such as social media, entrepreneurship, work-life balance, and international issues, all of which this text covers in detail, were not a focus for nurses as they are and should be today. The chapter on mentorship particularly resonated with me. Although I did not have access to the information and tools in this book, I was fortunate to have the guidance of mentors whose support paralleled these topic areas. The mentorship chapter addresses not only having a mentor but also being a mentor. Based on the support I received across my career, I purposefully focus on being a mentor and giving back. The authors provide details on both areas, including how to develop a strong, effective mentoring relationship.

At first glance, *Take Charge of Your Nursing Career* may appear to be just for new graduates; however, it is so much more. I highly recommend this rich, easy-to-read, practical book for nurses to use at all points on their journey. They will find guidance for success in their current positions and/or as they transition into new positions. Educators can also use this book in courses preparing students for graduation and their careers. In short, the important information in this book will help nurses be successful and therefore will make a difference for nursing and the health of those we provide care.

–Patricia Thompson, EdD

PREFACE. OR, SOME WORDS ON THE PANDEMIC . . .

Thanks to the COVID-19 pandemic, the period between March 2020 and March 2021, when this book was completed, has been one of the most impactful years of our lives. Every nurse across the globe has been affected personally and/or professionally in one way or another by the pandemic. Maybe you were a practicing nurse who had to quickly adapt to a changing work environment. Perhaps you were a nurse leader in a clinical setting charged with helping others navigate these uncharted waters. Possibly you were a nurse educator who had to reformulate your approach to teaching nursing students without in-person classroom or clinical experiences. Perhaps you had to work virtually—something new, strange, and stressful. Maybe you were a nurse in a rural area who was furloughed or laid off. Or maybe had to put your career on hold for family or other reasons.

Your life's path may have taken unexpected twists and turns this year. But as we emerge from the pandemic, each one of us should take a moment to assess where we are personally and professionally. Anytime a crisis of the magnitude of COVID-19 occurs, it's natural to take stock in this way. In doing so, you might realize that you are experiencing some degree of post-traumatic stress disorder. If so, it's critical that you take the time you need to heal, and to get help if you need it. Although you might have been repeatedly told you are a "healthcare hero," you might not feel that way. It's OK to take a minute to reestablish your personal and professional self! The nursing profession and all its diverse career options will still be here when you're ready to reemerge.

We have learned many lessons as individuals, communities, and a global society, as well as within the nursing profession. We can use these lessons—both positive and negative—to modify our short-term and long-term goals or even establish new ones as we move forward. For some of you, the immediate focus will be on personal goals. Others will focus on achieving existing career goals. Still others—especially those of you who have been on the front lines—might be considering a career realignment or a career change.

Not everyone wants change, let alone embraces it. But thinking ahead and being prepared for change are critical to your career journey. Change is not always easy, and it doesn't always happen right away. Still, one of the great things about being a nurse is that you can constantly re-examine your career trajectory and expand and grow in directions you hadn't even dreamed of when you graduated from nursing school. Particularly as our world regains its balance in the aftermath of the COVID 19 pandemic, be open to a new and different future. When you are ready to move forward—or even sideways—I hope you will allow this book to assist you in examining all the possibilities open to you as a professional nurse and determining how to make them happen for you.

Thank you for all you have done and continue to do during this pandemic. As a profession, we nurses have fought hard—enduring both failures and successes. Sometimes it felt as though we moved two steps forward and then five steps back. Eventually, though, we helped turn the tide. We made a difference. To me, that is the embodiment of nursing—making our unique impact, individually and collectively, for the people who depend on us.

INTRODUCTION

Your career is analogous to the birth of a butterfly—

From egg to caterpillar, you are nourished and learn to navigate your surroundings—

From larvae to butterfly, you self-reflect, and you prepare to take flight—

As the butterfly with courage, vibrancy, and excitement is ready to soar—

It is time to step into your career and make your unique difference—

Fly high, don't be inhibited to take changes in flight, and make your impact—

The nursing profession and you will be that much better by the difference you make.

This is the second edition of *Take Charge of Your Nursing Career*. Since the first edition was published in 2010 by Sigma Theta Tau International Honor Society of Nursing, the topic of career development and management, in all its many facets, has gained greater interest as a career-long process rather than something that only new graduates experience or that people consider when a new career opportunity becomes available. As the nursing profession continues to grow and evolve, professional nurses' career development and management must keep pace.

Sigma is leading in the effort globally to provide career development and management guidance to its members. Sigma's Career Center has a central presence at conferences, both in-person and virtually. The Career Center is the tent from which many opportunities flow, including but not limited to the Career Advice Forum on the Circle, many Sigma academies (which clearly focus on the expansion of one's career), and the various presentations delivered to assist members in their career growth.

The second edition of this book is another means of presenting (in a conversational, user-focused format) these topics that are so essential to developing, managing, and expanding one's career. The book also gives nurses—both members and non-members of Sigma—a "one-stop" career guide that addresses issues that will be relevant for the entirety of their career.

The essential theme of the book is the notion of career as a fluid process. A career is not stagnant or simply a job. It is a process that must be nurtured—constantly grown and managed. A career is an opportunity to find one's voice and use it to promote both the individual and professional impact of one's expertise. A career should be challenging, always giving way to more learning and mentoring opportunities. Career is a global concept; the intricacies of career development and management across the globe cannot be overlooked. A career journey ebbs and flows—one of the great characteristics of a professional nursing career. There are always options to consider on one's career path—opportunities to gain experience and expertise in diverse areas, often never considered by professional nurses.

Take Charge of Your Nursing Career provides the reader with a unique and distinct perspective on career development and management. It covers timely and relevant topics, strategies, tips, and examples for professional nurses to use to develop and manage their careers from beginning to end. It also provides resources and websites that they can access as needed as they define their personal career trajectory. The topics discussed throughout the book are ones that professional nurses at all points on their career journey are asking about and dealing with in their careers, now and in the future. Professional nurses can turn to this user-friendly book through the entirety of their career.

Much of this version of the book was written during the COVID-19 pandemic, which as of this writing continues to affect our daily lives. Not surprisingly, in the shadow of the pandemic, career development and management has taken on even more importance for nursing professionals. New graduates are entering a nursing workforce in which expectations have been expanded and are quite challenging. Many more experienced nurses have changed roles. Some nurses have seen their positions eliminated and are expected to change with the times, but without necessarily having the education, skill set, or "how to" approach needed to make those changes. *Take Charge of Your Nursing Career* addresses these issues and more.

The nursing profession and healthcare environment are different from when the first edition of this book was released. Today, nursing professionals across the globe and at each stage in their career consistently ask how to navigate, grow, and expand their careers; change their career trajectories; and develop, hone, and promote their nursing identities. Nursing professionals are focused on career-development and management areas that are far beyond writing a resumé or curriculum vitae. They are looking for career resources that apply to the many roles and challenges they face at all points and phases of their career. This book provides just that.

Each chapter begins with at least one vignette from a nurse I have met along my own career journey. These nurses reflect on something meaningful to them that relates to the focus of the corresponding chapter. The 11 chapters cover topics to help to nurses grow, maintain, sustain, and advance our careers. Chapters from the first edition have been updated and expanded to include content on resumés, curriculum vitae, portfolios, educational advancement, professional development, and entrepreneurship. In addition, this new edition of the book covers subjects that were not addressed in the first edition that are timely and relevant to the world in which we currently live and work. They include mentorship, developing your nursing identity, international nursing, the impact and use of social media in our careers, expanding your reach with your voice, and work-life balance.

Take Charge of Your Nursing Career, Second Edition meets the needs of *all* professional nurses. Finally, we have a book that addresses the issues we face and the tools we can use for our entire career! For example:

- Nursing students and new graduates can use this book to obtain resources for resumé development and interviewing. They can also use it in relation to the broader issue of their career development. For example, they can use the practical "hands-on" resources in this book to develop a career plan, to develop and manage a portfolio, and to market themselves. And they can obtain guidance on advancing their career through formal education and professional development.

- Professional nurses who have been in practice for 5 to 10 years can use this book to explore other opportunities within nursing and healthcare and to manage their career path and as they consider taking steps to alter their career trajectory. Practical information on what steps to take will be most helpful to these nurses as they consider new experiences to expand their careers.

- Mid-career nurses who want to change or advance their careers— perhaps by obtaining additional education, progressing to a more advanced nursing position, pursuing international opportunities, considering positions outside their comfort zone, or attempting entrepreneurship—will find information in this book that addresses their questions. Specific areas of interest to mid-career nurses include but are not limited to mentorship, finding their voice, and expanding their reach. Chapters that outline how to develop and maintain a resumé, curriculum vitae, and/or portfolio, and on marketing oneself (including behavioral interviewing), could also be of interest to this population of nurses, who may not have undergone such experiences earlier in their careers.

- Professional nurses who are late in their careers and may even have transitioned into retirement, but who want to continue to make a difference in the nursing profession by pursuing non-traditional nursing opportunities, will find applicable resources in this book. These include resources that pertain to mentorship and professional or political advocacy.

This book even addresses specific challenges facing international nurses—for example, obtaining licensure in the United States, practicing across the world, educational opportunities outside their home countries, and mentorship. There is much here for nurses who want to expand to a more global practice in diverse countries and regions of the world.

In other words, *all* professional nurses, no matter what point on their career journey, are the audience for *Take Charge of Your Nursing Career*. There is something for everyone, from the student to the new graduate, from the emerging-career to the mid-career nurse, to the later-career nurse. This readable, conversational, and practical book is for Sigma members and non-members, from all corners of the globe. It presents common questions, answers, and resources that nurses can use as they develop, manage, maintain, grow, advance, and elevate their careers.

Your career is a path will have ebbs and flows, winding roads and curves—sometimes expected, but often unexpected. Take each turn as a learning experience. Both positive *and* negative experiences provide us with valuable lessons that we can use as we manage our careers. As I learned on my own career journey, the unexpected change in a career path often turns out to be the best thing that could have happened to you—opening new doors, providing new and challenging experiences, and taking you to places you never imagined. I hope that as you read *Take Charge of Your Nursing Career*, you will find invaluable information that you can use as you travel your own career journey. I also hope that your journey is as full of excitement and fulfillment as mine has been.

Remember: No one individual travels their career journey alone. I certainly have not. So, reach out to others—including me if you need some guidance or advice. And always strive to be that butterfly that soars. Be willing to take and meet challenges, collaborate, disseminate, seek out experiences to grow and advance your career, and harness your uniqueness to make an impact that no one else could make in the exact same way.

I can't wait to see where your career journey takes you, and you take it!

–Lois

1

THE ART AND SCIENCE OF MARKETING YOURSELF

"I am often asked, why do I need to market myself? I am finally a nurse, and nurses are always needed. But as a new graduate, I cannot find the position I want as a nurse. No one even gives me an interview. No one seems to want to hire a new graduate. What am I doing wrong?"

–T. G., BSN, RN

"I am at a place in my career where I want to explore other options. I might not be ready to leave my current position, but how will I know what else might be a fit for me—something new, exciting, and challenging—if I do not look? How will a prospective employer know if I am the right fit for their organization?"

–J. R., BSN, CCRN, RN

THE WHY OF MARKETING

Nurses at all levels—from new graduates, to experienced or mid-career nurses, to experts in nursing entering the latter stages of their careers—must market themselves if they want to advance and/or change the direction of their career. This might mean sharing your unique qualities as a nurse in writing or through the interview process.

Making the case for why *you* are the best, most-qualified person for a particular position is essential, as no one else will do it for you—at least not initially. No matter where you are in your career journey, if you want to increase your chances of securing the position that is the best fit for you, you *must* employ the art and science of marketing.

WHERE DO I BEGIN?

If you are a soon-to-be-graduating nursing student or one who has recently graduated, the most important job for you is to graduate and successfully pass your licensure examination. Otherwise, marketing yourself for a first career position will be for naught. If you have passed your licensure examination and are an early-career nurse, a mid-career nurse, or a nurse who is in the latter stage of your career, then you can begin or advance your professional career in all the diverse ways that are available in nursing.

Depending on whether you are a new nurse or have already begun your career journey, and depending on the path you have taken up to this point in your career, the process of searching for a new position or opportunity will vary somewhat. But it is a process, nonetheless. Throughout this process, you must serve as your own public relations or marketing manager. It is critical that you market yourself—your abilities, expertise, and experience, and your potential contributions to an employer—always putting your best foot forward. No one knows you better than you do, so it is up to you to convince potential employers that they want you to work for them.

The first step in this process will often involve developing a resumé or curriculum vitae. A *resumé* is a document that contains facts about your career, usually in bullet-point format but without detailed explanatory text. Your resumé should be concise,

>
> **Note**
> The process of searching for a first nursing position or changing positions along your career path often begins well before you actively begin seeking a specific position.

succinct, and directed, highlighting information about you and your career that is key to the position for which you are applying. Typically, resumés are short in length—usually one to two pages, although yours could be longer if you are a more experienced nurse. Appendix A contains examples of resumés that you can use as a guide.

In contrast, a *curriculum vitae* (CV), which is typically longer in length, contains a more detailed and descriptive set of facts about your career history. Your CV might describe the responsibilities relating to a partic-
ular position you held, contain details about an award you received, or outline a presentation you delivered or a paper you published. In other words, the CV is a more comprehensive depiction of your professional career. Appendix B contains an example of a completed CV, and Appendix C has a blank one that you can use as a template to create your own.

> **Tip**
> When writing a resumé, the facts it contains should appear as a list. You can then use this list as the basis of your CV, simply adding a brief description for each list item that appears in your resumé. The CV can also be expanded to include additional categories.

Which type of document you should submit and what it should include depend on the type of nursing position you are pursuing. For example, if you are applying for a practice position at any level, you will most likely be asked to submit an updated resumé. If you are applying for a faculty position in an academic institution or a research position for a healthcare organization or governmental agency, you will more likely be required to submit a CV. For some nursing positions, whether you submit a resumé or a CV might depend on how long you've worked in the nursing profession or some other distinguishing characteristic. The bottom line is that the documentation requirements will vary from position to position and from employer to employer. So, your best course of action will be to know what both types of documents are and what they include, and to determine how to effectively present yourself as a nursing professional in each format. That way, you'll be ready for anything!

Not all regions or countries require the same type of documentation for the same position. Be sure you know what specifically is required in the region or country where you are applying for a position. Also, be aware that in the United Kingdom and parts of Europe, the term *CV* is used more broadly to include what we might call a resumé, while the term *resumé* is generally *not* used. In contrast, in South Africa, Australia, and India, the terms *CV* and *resumé* are used interchangeably. It's a good idea to ask the human resources department (or equivalent) of the organization where you are hoping to gain a position—be it a clinical organization, a university, or other healthcare-related entity—about their expectations with regard to what type of career documentation you submit. Doing your due diligence ahead of time can help you get your foot in the door for the career position you are interested in obtaining!

GENERAL THOUGHTS ON RESUMÉS AND CVS

A resumé and CV represent you as a professional registered nurse and provide a historical perspective of your career to this point. They should reflect the best of you. For prospective employers, your resumé or CV serves to make a first impression. It is critical that this first impression be a great one!

Tip

Think of your resumé or CV as you in business attire on paper. Just as you would not go to a job interview in jeans and a T-shirt, you should not submit a resumé that looks casual. You want to make a lasting first impression on a potential employer—and you want that impression to be positive. This first impression can make all the difference for your career progress.

Employers look at hundreds of resumés for varied and diverse positions,
and perhaps even more at certain
times of the year, such as when nursing
students graduate. Knowing this, your
goal is for your resumé to *stand out*
(but not in a bad way). You want your

> **Note**
> Many employers in the United
> States—especially clinical
> organizations—generally pre-
> fer to receive resumés rather
> than CVs, especially as a first
> method of contact.

resumé—how it is put together and what it says about you—to stick
with the reader. You don't want it to end up in a pile of maybes or, even
worse, in a pile of no's, which will likely end up being deleted from the
employer's computer system or thrown into the literal garbage can.

Resumés can be submitted via email, via snail mail, or hand-delivered if
you have a collegial relationship with the hiring individual or someone
with influence on the hiring process. But it is much more common today
for resumés to be submitted through an online system. Many organizations use an automatic tracking system (ATS) to sift through resumés in
a more efficient manner. These systems often rely on keywords to match
resumés with job openings. Although it's a good idea to know what
keywords you should include in your resumé, don't focus too much on
this. If you compose your resumé thinking only about what keywords
the ATS might be looking for, there's a good chance your resumé will be
rejected for being "too perfect."

> **Tip**
> Don't second guess yourself when it comes to what keywords to include
> on your resumé. Use certain keywords if they apply to your qualifications
> but don't try and fit them in just to cater to the ATS. Submit a resumé that
> reflects you and what you have done in your career, even if you are a new
> graduate.

While you shouldn't try too hard to stuff your resumé with keywords,
you *should* target it to reflect the job description for the position for
which you are applying. The same goes for your CV. For example, if a
job description contains specific requirements—for example, advanced
cardiac life support or certification in chemotherapy—be sure to include

those in your resumé or CV. Otherwise, in the case of a resumé, the ATS will block your resumé from moving forward in the selection process. In a similar vein, some applications contain questions, like, "Do you have experience in cardiac life support?" or "Are you certified to administer chemotherapy?" If you answer no to these questions, your application will not advance. (These types of questions are called *knock-out questions*.)

Note

If the organization where you are applying asks you to include specific information or other items in your resumé or CV, be sure to include (or address) them. Ignoring these requirements will serve as a red flag for the hiring organization and may prevent your resumé from moving forward in the process. They may conclude that if you can't follow directions when submitting your resumé or CV, you probably won't follow directions in your position.

The ATS—and eventually the person who reads your resumé—looks for information presented in a "fact format" that relates to hard skills and soft skills you possess. *Hard skills* are those skills that are learned through education and specialized training or practice. These are primarily the psychomotor and cognitive skills you need to perform your responsibilities in your position—for example, assessment, patient and family education, safety, and emergency care. *Soft skills* relate to personal characteristics and are often described (although not solely) as part of the affective domain. You gain and develop these skills over a career and lifetime of experiences. Some examples include communication, critical thinking, time management, empathy, teamwork, ethics, and confidentiality. This does not mean you should simply include lists of skills-related keywords on your resumé. Instead, you should integrate this type of information into bullet points under a position you have held or in your cover letter (if this is acceptable to the employer). Again, if the job description calls for any specific skills and you have those skills, be sure to mention them in your resumé.

> **Note**
>
> The more experience you have as a professional nurse, the less you will need to focus on selling yourself as a new graduate. You will be able to use your knowledge, skills, and expertise that you have developed and refined in the "real world" environment in whatever positions you have held to market yourself through your resumé or CV.

When writing your resumé, don't be modest or hold back on what you can bring to an organization. No two nursing professionals have the same qualities. We are all framed by our experiences—both within the profession and outside it. It is these unique qualities, characteristics, and experiences, in addition to your history in the profession, that make you the nursing professional you are. Be sure to highlight your uniqueness! Show prospective employers what you could bring to their organization and why you are right for the position for which they are hiring. Make them think, "If I don't hire this person, my organization will be losing out."

It's a good idea to generate several versions of your resumé or CV, targeting each one for a particular position or organization. For example, if you are a new graduate and completed some of your clinical work at an agency where you are now applying for a position, you should include those clinical experiences on a targeted resumé or CV for that organization. If you are a more seasoned nurse who has helped educate nurses at all levels of your organization, and you are now applying for a position as a clinical instructor or a full-time faculty member, include those educational experiences in your resumé or CV. This will convey that although you might not have academic teaching experience, you do have experience educating nurses, and you consider this to be a transferable skill that you could build on. As an added bonus, tailoring your resumé or CV in this way lets the reader know that you have done your research on the position for which you are applying.

Your resumé or CV should contain no spelling or grammatical errors. Even if you use a spell/grammar check tool, be sure to reread it yourself (or have someone else do it for you) to ensure that no errors were missed. If your resumé or CV has errors, it reflects poorly on you. It can even serve as a red flag for your potential employer, taking you out of the running for the position for which you are applying—even if you're the best person for the job. Also, you should use a readable font size— usually 11 or 12 point—and make sure your entries are aligned. Finally, even though your resumé or CV might be submitted via an online application system, you will still need to print copies of it to bring with you in the event you land an interview. Your best bet is to print your resumé or CV on professional, non-decorative paper, usually ivory, white, or beige in color.

> *Note*
>
> Some organizations have strict requirements with respect to formatting and submitting your resumé or CV. Be sure you follow them!

GETTING HELP WITH YOUR RESUMÉ OR CV

Many career nurses, no matter what stage they are in their career, have never written a formal resumé, so don't be embarrassed or afraid to ask for help from someone you trust. Have a friend or colleague who has more experience than you read through your resumé to be sure it is making the points—and impression—that you want it to.

In addition to seeking help from others, you can obtain assistance from various resources, such as those found at the Sigma Career Center or on various career-building websites. In addition, many word-processing programs, such as Microsoft Word, offer resumé templates that you can use as a guide.

Just remember: You are marketing yourself as a professional nurse based on your experience and expertise, not on your skill in writing a resumé. You want your resumé to be *yours*—reflecting your unique skills and characteristics.

THE COMPONENTS OF A RESUMÉ

Following is an overview of the components that you might include in your resumé. Not all these components will need to appear in everyone's resumé. Conversely, there might be components that aren't listed here that are unique to your career journey that you should include in your resumé.

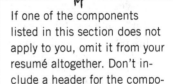

Tip

If one of the components listed in this section does not apply to you, omit it from your resumé altogether. Don't include a header for the component with no text underneath.

GOAL OR OBJECTIVE STATEMENT

Your goal or objective statement should not describe a career objective. Rather, it should be written specifically for the position for which you are applying and use similar wording to what appears in the position's job description. For example:

- If you are applying for an advanced practice position, your goal statement could express a desire to manage the comprehensive healthcare needs of patients and families.

- If you are applying for an administrative position in a clinical facility, your goal statement could address your commitment to work collaboratively with members of the nursing and healthcare team to promote the organization's goals.

- If you are a new graduate applying for a residency program, you could include specific words in the position posting in your goal statement—for example, "Having worked as a care technician in pediatrics for four years, I am seeking to join the Pediatrics Nurse Residency Program at [name of clinical agency] and build on my previous experience to work with diverse children and families across the health-illness continuum."

- If you are a more experienced nurse, you could write a goal statement that reflects your work and how it has prepared you to work in the position you are now seeking—for example, "I am a CCRN seeking an ER position at [name of clinical agency]. I bring 16 years of experience in a Level 2 Trauma Center at a county hospital with additional experience as a night manager at the same ER for the past two years. I am seeking a position where I can use my skills, knowledge, and clinical expertise in a larger country hospital and/or a Level 1 Trauma Center."

> **Tip**
>
> Specificity is key here. If you can only come up with generalities—for example, "I am looking for a new graduate position," or, "I am looking to move up the career ladder"—then it's better to omit the goal/objective statement from your resumé.

LICENSURE AND CERTIFICATION

This section should include your registered nurse licensing information. This includes the following:

- Your license number (if recommended by the potential employer)

- The dates the license is valid

- Whether you have an advanced practice license

- Whether your license is from a single state or from a state that is a member of the Nurse Licensure Compact

> **Note**
>
> You do not need to include licenses that have expired or are inactive.

There is some debate about whether to include your license number on your resumé. While applicants might be concerned that their identity could be stolen, individuals who work in HR departments are bound by strict ethical and legal policies, standards, rules, and regulations—meaning that it is highly unlikely they would commit such a transgression.

Besides, these HR professionals can easily obtain the information in question by searching the state licensure database for nurses (assuming you inform them of the type of license you hold and the state that issued it). If you're not sure whether to include it, follow the hiring organization's recommendation. If no recommendation is given, then whether you include your license number is up to you. (For what it's worth, I do include my license number on my documentation.)

You should also list information about any certifications you hold in this section of your resumé. This includes:

- Your certification number

- The granting agency

- The dates during which the certification is valid

Obtaining certifications (and listing them on your resumé) is one way to differentiate your resumé from those of others applying for the same position. For example, if you are a new graduate seeking your first position in an intensive care unit, you could obtain certification in advanced cardiac life support before applying for the position and include that certification on your resumé. This will show that you are a self-starter, are committed to advancing your knowledge and skills in the area in which you want to work, and are willing to pay for your certification rather than wait for a clinical organization to cover the cost—all of which will highlight your uniqueness as a professional nurse.

Note

If you are a new nurse, becoming certified in a skill or subject that is relevant to the area of nursing you want to pursue will make you much more marketable!

Tip

If you are a more experienced nurse who wants to switch to a different area of nursing, try searching through professional journals or websites for professional organizations that coincide with your new area of interest to see what types of relevant certifications are available.

EDUCATION

In this section of your resumé, you cite your educational experience, from most recent to least recent. This information should include:

- The name of the college or university you attended

- The city and state in which the school is located

- The years you attended

- The degree conferred

- The year in which the degree was granted

Do not include in this list coursework that did not result in the granting of a degree—even if you completed it to meet prerequisites for the degree you ultimately received. Also omit coursework you've completed to meet continuing education requirements. (You can include this information in the "Professional Activities" section of your resumé or, if you are a more experienced nurse, you can add a "Continuing Education" section and add it there.)

Remember, your resumé should set you apart from others. So, for example, if you also have a degree in business and are applying for an administrative position in nursing, you should include that information on your resumé. Or, if you have another degree in music or music therapy and your goal is to work with pediatric patients or adult cancer patients, then you should include *that* information on your resumé— perhaps briefly explaining how you would use music to enhance the care you would provide.

If you studied abroad while seeking your degree, you can include that as a bullet point in this section. The same goes for any honors or awards you received—for example, president's list, dean's list, summa cum laude, etc.

> **Note**
>
> You can also discuss your unique educational experiences in more detail in your cover letter and/or during your interview.

Alternatively, you can list honors and awards in a separate section. (More on this in a minute.)

EXPERIENCE

There is no one way to complete this section. You can present your information in a couple different ways:

- List all your experiences, from most recent to least recent, in a single section.

- Divide your experience into subsections—for example:

    - Clinical Experience (if you are a graduating nurse)

    - Nursing Experience (other than clinical)

    - Related Healthcare Experience (for positions in healthcare but not in nursing)

    - Other Work Experience (for all other types of work experience)

> **Tip**
>
> How you structure this section depends on the experiences you have had, how important they are to your professional growth, and their potential impact on the position for which you are applying.

Regardless of how you structure this section, you'll want to include the following information for each position or job you have held:

- The name of the place of employment

- The city and state in which the place of employment is located

- The years you worked for the organization

- Your job title (e.g., charge nurse, nurse manager, and so on)

- One or two bullet points to describe your work responsibilities (if necessary)

You can also include bullet points to detail the type of facility you worked at, the number of beds on your unit, the type of patients you treated, and so on.

Tip

Don't worry about time gaps in your experiences. In nursing, it's understood that we might have gaps in our employment due to family obligations, returning to school, and so on. Your resumé will be viewed for what it says about your career up to this point as a nursing professional, not for whether you consistently worked with no gaps in time.

Notice I said you needed to provide a description of your work responsibilities "if necessary." To elaborate, if the person who will be reading your resumé likely knows what the position or job entails, you need not include this description, even in bullet form. It is redundant to tell the reader what they already know. It also saves space on your resumé for more relevant details. For example, if you were a charge nurse at a regional hospital, you would not need to describe what you did there unless it involved some responsibility that was out of the ordinary. The same goes if you worked as, say, a barista—a position in which you gained important customer-service and communication skills that could transfer to nursing. On the other hand, if you were a test item writer for a certification examination, then you *would* want to explain your duties because the person reading your resumé might not be familiar with them.

New nurse graduates often ask whether they should include all their clinical experiences during nursing school on their resumé. Here's my advice: Find out if you live in a state or want to work for a clinical agency that requires you to list your clinical experiences and the hours completed on your resumé. If so, then include them. If not, just cite your preceptorship, capstone, or practicum experience on your resumé, as this will differentiate you from other new nurse graduates applying for the same position. You should also cite any clinical experience requirements you've fulfilled at the organization where you are submitting your resumé. You might not think it would make a difference, but if it sets you apart from other applicants, it could be what gets you hired.

You are not limited to citing work experiences in nursing or healthcare. You can also include other types of work experiences—especially if you are a recent nurse graduate or a relatively new nurse. Note, however, that it's best to focus on work experiences that involved skills that are transferrable to nursing—for example, for a business or in the military; as a translator, a legal expert, or a consultant; in management; and so on. You can also include positions you held for long periods of time (at least one year). Remember: We all gain experience from a wide variety of positions, and these are important to who you are as a nursing professional.

Tip
After you have moved past the new nurse stage, you should remove clinical experiences from your resumé completely, as now you have experience as a professional nurse.

Note
Customer service, communication, budgeting, and leadership are examples of skills that translate well to nursing.

HONORS AND AWARDS

You use this section to cite nursing-related honors and awards you received in school (assuming you didn't already include them in the "Education" section of your resumé) or that were bestowed upon you by a clinical or professional organization during your professional career as a nurse. This includes being inducted into Sigma (if applicable); be sure to cite your induction date and the chapter into which you were inducted.

Tip
Be sure you include the exact name of the honor or award you received and the date you received it.

This section can also include scholarships you received while pursuing your undergraduate and/or graduate education. If you received multiple scholarships, highlight the ones that are academic in nature, from better-known granting agencies, or involved higher amounts of funds.

Finally, this section can include honors or awards in areas other than nursing—especially if they are well-known honors or awards and you earned them during your professional career. This helps show the breadth of your work experience.

> *Tip*
> If you have not received any honors or awards, leave this section off your resumé.

PROFESSIONAL ORGANIZATIONS AND ACTIVITIES

This is an especially important component to prospective employers. It shows that you are engaged in the profession—that nursing is not just a job to you, but a career in which you are participating at varied levels. It also reveals your level of professional, leadership, and service growth. The longer you have been in your career, the more significant this section becomes. So, make sure you include not only the organizations to which you belong and your dates of membership, but also bullet points listing any offices you've held and any conferences you've attended.

PRESENTATIONS AND PUBLICATIONS

In this section, you want to cite any presentations (poster and/or podium) that you have given as a professional nurse. Include the following information:

- The title of the presentation

- Whether it was a poster or podium presentation

- The name of the organization that accepted your abstract or requested the presentation

- Where the presentation took place (including if it was a virtual presentation)

For publications, list any relevant articles or other pieces that you may have published, including but not limited to the following:

BEWARE PREDATORY JOURNALS

You should only publish in reputable journals or other publications. If you published in a predatory journal—even if you did so at the time unknowingly—do not list it on your resumé.

With the increased movement toward open-access journals, there has also been an increase in the number of predatory journals, particularly online. This is not unique to nursing or healthcare. Fortunately, there are sites that can assist you in finding out if the journal you may be interested in publishing in is reputable. For example, the International Academy of Nursing Editors maintains a list of reputable journals called the "Nursing Journal Directory." Journals in this directory are vetted before they are included. You can find information about the directory, as well as a direct link to it, here: https://nursingeditors.com/journals-directory.

It also helps to be aware of red flags. For example, the editor of a reputable journal will never contact you to ask you to pay a fee upfront to publish an article. Promises of rapid review and acceptance are also suspect, as are mass emails that invite submissions.

- Scientific nursing research

- Evidence-based studies/translational research

- Quality-improvement projects

- Systematic reviews and meta-analyses

- Integrative reviews

- Concept analyses

- Research monographs

- Columns

- White papers

Be sure to indicate where your publication was published and if it was

Tip

If you are a new nurse graduate, only list presentations or publications that were outside of your course activities or requirements.

peer-reviewed. You might also want to indicate whether your publication is open access.

COMMUNITY OR VOLUNTEER SERVICE

This section should list service projects or experiences in which you have participated—especially those related to the type of position you are seeking. For example, if you want to obtain a nursing position on an oncology unit and you have participated in community-service activities to help raise money for cancer-related causes, you should put that on your resumé. The same goes for any mission trips you've taken that related to the provision of healthcare.

> **Tip**
>
> Do not list every service activity you have ever participated in. This looks like you are padding your resumé, which is a red flag to the reader. Be selective when including the facts of your service activities.

SPECIAL SKILLS AND/OR EXPERTISE

Use this section to list unique skills or expertise that might be important to someone who is seeking to fill the position for which you are applying. This should not be a listing of common skills—like PowerPoint or Excel—but of skills that might make you more marketable than someone else. For instance, are you multilingual? If so, in what languages? Do you speak and/or write those languages? If so, you will be able to provide a service to some patients that other candidates might not be capable of doing. As another example, do you have experience using electronic medical records systems? If so, which ones? If you are familiar with the system that your prospective employer uses, they will not have to train you, which makes you a more desirable candidate. Finally, do you have experience with budgeting or art

> **Tip**
>
> Don't include items in this section just for the sake of doing so. This could actually hurt your chances with a prospective employer. If you don't have relevant and unique skills and/or expertise, just leave this section off your resumé.

and/or music therapy? Again, these skills might give you an edge over other candidates

REFERENCES

If you have room at the bottom of your resumé, you can add the statement, "References available upon request." This is not necessary, however—especially if you do not have room for them.

When choosing references, select people who will give prospective employers honest and positive feedback about you and what you will contribute to a position. References can include your colleagues, subordinates, superiors, or personal contacts. Make sure you ask the person in advance to serve as a reference for you and obtain their contact information, including their email address and phone number. Do not include their names and contact information on your resumé. This information should be on a separate page that accompanies your resumé.

BUILDING A CURRICULUM VITAE

As you've learned, a resumé is a fact-based document that details information about either your entire career or career highlights that relate to the position(s) for which you are applying. Similarly, a curriculum vitae (CV) is a concise summary of your career experience, but with more details, in the form of bullet points or short explanations.

Often, prospective employers request a CV for an academic, research, leadership, or similar position, or from an individual with many years of experience/expertise. A CV might also be requested by a grant-funding agency or if you are applying for a fellowship.

Note

A CV should include more details than a resumé, but less than a portfolio. Portfolios are discussed in Chapter 2, "Your Career Repository: The Portfolio."

A CV generally includes similar components to a resumé, including the following:

- Educational and academic background

- Professional experience

- Honors and awards

- Presentations and publications

- Professional organizations and activities

It could also contain additional components, such as the following:

- Leadership experience

- Teaching experience

- Research

- Grants received

- Service organizations

You can certainly modify these components as needed so they apply to your career. You can include subheads within certain categories—for example, in the "Presentation" section, you might include subheads for international, national, state, or local presentations. Use your own creative judgement to make the best case for your career journey within the confines of a CV.

If you have never created a CV before, or you want to create a CV for a specific type of position, you can find plenty of information and resources to assist you. For example, you can visit websites for professional organizations, such as Sigma Theta Tau International. (Search in the Career

Tip

Even if you are a more experienced nurse, don't feel that you should have already created a CV or that you should even know how to develop one. Just like anything else, there is a first time for everything, even if it is later in your career.

Center.) You can also inquire with the agency, organization, or institution where you are planning to submit your CV to see if they have a particular format they want you to use, or perhaps check their website for examples to serve as a guide. Using their preferred format demonstrates that you have done the appropriate research on their guidelines prior to submission.

ABCS OF RESUMÉ/CV DEVELOPMENT

A   Accurate

B   Brief

C   Clear

D   Directed (toward position)

E   Encapsulating

F   Fact-Based

INTRODUCING YOURSELF IN A COVER LETTER

Unlike a resumé or CV, a cover letter is not usually required when you apply for a job. However, if you are able to submit one, you can use a cover letter to supplement those required documents. In other words, you can use the cover letter to introduce yourself to a prospective employer, identify the position for which you are applying, and explain why you are the best person for that position. But don't just *say* you are the ideal candidate; cite specific information about your professional and/or personal life to *prove* that you are.

Your cover letter should be brief—no longer than one page—but written in such a way that it grabs the reader's attention. The idea is to compose a cover letter that is compelling enough to garner an interview with the potential employer. Appendix D contains two sample cover letters.

THE INTERVIEW: IT GOES BOTH WAYS

When you submit your resumé or CV and possibly a compelling cover letter, your goal is to be granted an interview with the potential employer.

There are varying types of interviews. These include:

- **In-person interviews:** Although these have been less common in recent years due to the COVID-19 pandemic, they will likely occur more often once the pandemic has abated. In any case, if you are interviewing in person, you must dress professionally, in business attire. For more information, see the upcoming sidebar, "Charting Your Career: General Tips for Interviews."

- **Virtual interviews:** These days, especially due to the COVID-19 pandemic, more and more interviews are conducted virtually using Zoom, Skype, or some other similar technology. Virtual interviews also enable prospective employers to interview candidates who do not currently live in their geographical area. If you are being interviewed virtually, not only do you need to dress professionally, but the area of your environment that will be seen on camera should be clean and without distractions, too. For more information, see the upcoming sidebar, "Charting Your Career: Virtual Interview Tips."

- **Phone interviews:** As with a virtual interview, during a phone interview, you want to be sure you have a good phone connection, whether on a land line or a cellular device. Also, you want to situate yourself in a quiet environment where you will not be interrupted. When the interview begins, make sure both parties can hear each other well and that there is no static or other noise on the line. During the interview, speak clearly. Finally, if the interviewer says something during the interview that you do not understand, simply ask for clarification.

No matter what type of interview you do, remember: It is not just the potential employer that is interviewing you; you are interviewing them, too. Make sure during the interview process that the organization is the best fit for you, just as they are determining whether you are the best person for them.

> **Tip**
> Interviewing is a two-way process, and listening is as important as responding.

DOING YOUR HOMEWORK: PREPARING FOR YOUR INTERVIEW

For many of us, interviewing is an inherently stressful process. Whether you are a new graduate nurse or a nurse with 20 years of experience (or more!), interviewing for a new position can increase your anxiety. To relieve this anxiety, you must arrive at the interview as prepared as possible.

To prepare for your interview, you will want to research several topics:

- **The available position:** You want to track down specific information about the available position. Find out how the organization describes the position and responsibilities. This will enable you to ask appropriate questions for clarification when you have the opportunity.

- **The organization:** Be a "detective." Check out the organization's website. Read all you can about the organization in newspapers, journals, and other sources. Finally, talk to any employees you might know who currently work there to get a sense of the organization's reputation and activities that might not be obvious to an outsider. This will help you decide how committed you are to obtaining the position.

- **The population served:** This could be patients, students, the community, or some other group. Find out who you would be serving and influencing (if you land the position) and whether you would do so through direct patient care, education, research, or something similar.

CHARTING YOUR CAREER: GENERAL TIPS FOR INTERVIEWS

- Practice ahead of time by answering commonly asked questions. The best way to do this is to simulate an actual interview with a peer or mentor. You might even want to record your practice session so you can watch it and identify any quirks or habits to avoid. Practicing ahead of time will give you a sense of confidence and comfort when you are in the real interview.

- Be on time. In fact, be 15 minutes early.

- Bring all requested materials with you, including hard copies of your resumé or CV, your transcript, your portfolio, handouts for presentations (if applicable), and so on.

- Carry a notepad or something similar to take notes during the interview.

- Be prepared for what has been scheduled for you. This will likely differ depending on the job you are interviewing for. For example:

  - **Clinical nurses:** Interview with one or more leadership individuals and tour the facility. (Be sure to bring scrubs or a lab coat, depending on what they recommend.)

  - **Faculty:** Interview with administration, faculty, and university personnel, and deliver a presentation to faculty on a research/evidence-based project.

  - **Administration:** Interview with upper administration and deliver a presentation related to strategies for improvement/change.

  - **Researcher:** Interview with prospective colleagues/administration, deliver a presentation on your research, and discuss grants/funding received.

- Bring list of questions to ask the interviewer(s) related to the position, responsibilities, a typical day at work, the chain of command, evaluation policies/procedures, and anything else you think is relevant.

- Be yourself, be honest, and don't forget to breathe!

CHARTING YOUR CAREER: VIRTUAL INTERVIEW TIPS

- Do not use a background if it appears pixelated. This can be distracting for the interviewer.

- If you cannot use a background, be sure that walls and surrounding areas are clean and professional in appearance. If you cannot remove pictures (or other items) from the wall behind you, either move to a different location with a plain wall or ensure that the pictures are not offensive or too personal.

- Make sure any phones you are not using are turned off or silenced.

- Don't conduct the interview in an area where noise can be heard, even if the noise is coming from outside.

- Check your device's connection ahead of time to decrease any chance of being disconnected during the interview process.

- If you have pets, keep them away from your area. You don't want your interview to be interrupted by a barking dog, a cat jumping into your lap in camera range, or any other lovable, but unprofessional, pet behaviors.

THE INTERVIEW PROCESS

As you know, the interview process generally involves answering a series of questions. These days, no matter what type of position you are interviewing for, most interview questions are behavioral questions. These are used to predict future behavior and performance based on past behavior and performance. When responding to behavioral questions:

- Describe a specific situation. It could be either a professional example or a personal one.

- Identify any hindrances, obstacles, or challenges you faced.

- Explain the action taken.

- Discuss the results or outcomes.

- Evaluate or summarize what you learned.

> **Tip**
>
> Again, it's a good idea to practice before you interview.

Typically, the process begins with an interview with a human resources representative. These types of interviews are more general in nature and are typically used to identify candidates who should move on to the next step of the interview process. Examples of these general types of questions include:

- Why did you choose to become a nurse?

- What is your overall experience(s) as a student/professional nurse?

- What are some examples of your specific job experiences, health-related or not?

- What are your strengths and weaknesses?

- How well do you work with others in a team setting? Please give examples.

- What attributes do you possess that make you the best candidate for this position?

> **Tip**
>
> The questions presented here are simply examples. Not all of these questions will apply to everyone. For example, the interviewer will likely ask a new graduate nurse a different set of questions than an experienced nurse, and the questions posed to a clinical nurse would be different from the questions asked of someone applying to a leadership, academic, or other position.

If you move to the next phase of the process, you may be asked to interview with a group of nurse managers (if you are seeking a clinical position), a group of faculty members (if it's an academic position you're after), or even a group of individuals in leadership positions in and out of nursing (for a variety of positions).

New graduates or early-career nurses might be asked questions that focus on their ability to problem-solve, prioritize, and/or delegate appropriately. These questions could focus on the specific patient population on the unit with the available position. You might also be asked how practicing in school differs from working as a new or early-career nurse.

In contrast, experienced nurses who have worked or want to work in various diverse areas might be asked some of the following questions:

- What management or leadership experience do you have?

- What experience do you have in academics/research/practice/policymaking?

- Where do you see your career in the next five or 10 years?

- How have your career goals changed over time as a professional nurse?

- What do you have to offer our organization/institution?

- Why should we hire you?

When interviewers want to use your past behavior to predict your future performance, they will often ask questions that include the phrase, "Give me some examples." For these types of questions, it is critical to describe a specific instance in which you demonstrated a particular behavior or skill that applies to the position for which you are being interviewed. (Remember: You can use professional or personal examples to illustrate the behavior in question.) Here are some examples:

- Give an example of when you experienced conflict and describe how you resolved the issue.

- Give an example of when you went above and beyond what was expected.

- Give an example of when you were a success.

- Give an example of when you anticipated a problem and how you influenced a change in direction or policy.

- Give an example of a time that you failed and how you handled that failure.

- Give an example of when you observed a co-worker violating the standards/expectations of their position. What action did you take? What did you base those actions on?

- Describe a time when you got in over your head on a project. How did you handle this?

- How would you handle a disrespectful colleague or an uncivil situation?

> **Tip**
> Answer all interview questions succinctly. Don't ramble or get off track.

CHARTING YOUR CAREER: OUT OF BOUNDS INTERVIEW QUESTIONS

Not all questions are appropriate in an interview setting. Indeed, asking some of these questions is downright illegal. Here are a few questions you are not obligated to answer. If you are asked one of these questions, it is perfectly acceptable to state, "I respectfully decline to answer that question."

- What is your marital status?
- What is your age?
- What is your sexual orientation or gender status?
- What is your religious affiliation?
- Do you have any chronic medical conditions/disabilities?

CONCLUDING THE INTERVIEW PROCESS

At the conclusion of the interview, thank the interviewer, whether in person or on the phone or a device screen. Then send a more formal thank you—either as a handwritten letter or in an email. You want to show gratitude to the interviewer for their time and for giving you the opportunity to interview for the position.

If the interviewer has asked you for additional documents or a proposal of some type, let them know in your more formal thank you communication that those will arrive under a separate email (or in whatever format they requested). Also let the interviewer know that you can be contacted via phone and/or email if they have further questions.

Tip

No matter how you correspond with the interviewer, make sure you use their appropriate title and credentials when addressing them.

Tip

If you interviewed with more than one person, send a thank you to all of those individuals if possible.

It is acceptable to express interest in similar positions if the position for which you applied is not a good fit for either of you or if it is no longer available. Close the correspondence by again thanking the interviewer and letting them know that you look forward to hearing from them at their earliest convenience.

2

YOUR CAREER REPOSITORY: THE PORTFOLIO

With Contributing Author Matthew S. Howard, DNP, RN, CEN, TCRN, CPEN, CPN

"I have just applied for a new position as a nurse administrator in a new organization. One of the requests from my interviewer was to provide a copy or link to my portfolio. At first, I was a little perplexed because they had my updated resumé. But when I asked them about it, they clarified that they would like to see my portfolio in addition to my resumé. Of course, I agreed to provide my portfolio, and then I panicked. I did not have a portfolio and did not know how long it would take to put one together or even where to start. I had Post-it Notes all over my house that noted presentations I had made at conferences or meetings I had attended, but not much else. What is the point of having a resumé if they want a portfolio, too? I am not applying for an academic position."

–D. C., MSN, RN

WHY A CAREER PORTFOLIO?

One of the most important things you can do for your career is to develop and maintain a career portfolio. A career portfolio is a repository of your life's professional work. Specifically, it consists of a set of documents that serve as evidence of your career achievements—from its inception to present-day—all in one place. These documents might include your resumé or CV, school transcripts, licenses and certifications, honors and awards, and so on. But that's not all. Your portfolio will also include narrative sections that allow you to present your career experience in more detail. Your career portfolio reveals your multifaceted experiences as a professional nurse and provides depth and perspective beyond what can be seen in a resumé or CV. Simply put, your career portfolio tells the story of your career.

> **Note**
>
> Your career portfolio is a set of documents that serve as evidence to support your achievements in your career. It also communicates your career identity and personality, reveals your uniqueness as a professional nurse, and highlights the best and most authentic version of you!

A career portfolio is essential. As you travel your career path, many individuals and/or groups may ask you for your portfolio or for some form of evidence of your career activities. Having all your relevant documentation in a single repository can help you advance your career—especially when timeliness is a factor. Interestingly, portfolios have led to higher retention and success rates for graduating students (Madden et al., 2019). The bottom line is that portfolios should be used by all practicing and professional nurses in all the diverse areas in which they work.

Portfolios can be used for a variety of purposes. For example:

- **To obtain a new career position:** This could be in any of the varied and diverse areas available to nursing professionals.

- **As part of a performance evaluation in your current position:** Portfolios can be used to assess a nurse's cognitive, reflective, and affective skills (Green et al., 2014). They can also be used to show your employer what you have done within your career outside your current job.

- **As part of the mentoring process:** When you enter a mentoring relationship, your mentor can use your portfolio—or components of it—to determine who you are as a nursing professional and what you want the mentoring relationship to accomplish.

- **To obtain a specialty certification:** Collecting detailed evidence of what you have accomplished in your career can be beneficial here. Often, certification bodies need documentation to prove your eligibility; having your portfolio on hand will enable you to access and provide it in an easy and timely manner.

- **To advance your formal education:** You'll need to provide documentation—such as transcripts, licenses and certifications, writing samples, and so on—when applying to programs to advance your education. Gathering this information into a portfolio expedites the process.

> **Note**
> Portfolios offer a space—either physical or electronic—for you to sustain your development as a nursing professional (St.-Germain et al., 2019).

It's not enough to develop a portfolio. You must also keep it up to date. Your portfolio is fluid; as such, it should be edited and updated as you travel your career path. Keep this in mind as you develop your portfolio. You want it to be easy to maintain!

> **Tip**
> As with resumés and CVs, it's a good idea to assemble multiple versions of your portfolio to target specific opportunities or organizations.

Many nursing professionals have what I call *Post-it portfolios*. They jot down what they have done in their career on a Post-it Note (or something similar) but never transfer these "moments in time" into a form that can be transmittable when needed. The idea that you can just throw everything together when someone asks for information from you about your career is shortsighted and will provoke stress when, suddenly, you need to complete this very task in a short turnaround. If you have not yet assembled a portfolio for your career, now is the time to do so. This chapter will show you how.

YOUR PORTFOLIO "FILE CABINET": THE COMPONENTS OF A PORTFOLIO

Think of your portfolio like a filing cabinet. Each drawer in the cabinet has specific sections that apply to your journey, and each section contains individual components that tell your story. These components are linked together by your career history. (See Figure 2.1.)

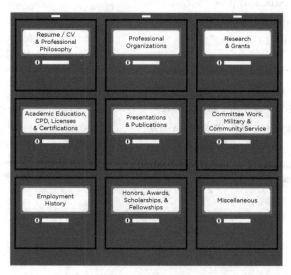

FIGURE 2.1   Your portfolio is like a filing cabinet filled with information about your journey and story.

So, what are the components in each drawer? It depends. Some components are universal, while others will be unique to you and your career. The following sections offer an overview of common portfolio components. Your

> **Tip**
> If you see a component in this section that does not apply to you or your career, simply leave it out of your portfolio.

portfolio might not include all these components. Additionally, you might think of other components for your portfolio that are unique to your career journey that don't appear here.

PRESENTING YOUR PORTFOLIO

There are various ways to present your career portfolio. For example, you can present your documents in a paper format, as an online e-portfolio, or using a hybrid or combination format. (The contents of your portfolio remain the same, regardless of what format you use.)

How you present your portfolio depends on what works best for you. Remember: It will be up to you to maintain your portfolio—updating its contents as you continue along your career path. If you choose a format that you are not comfortable using, you might be less likely to do this! Of course, if you're set on using a particular format but you're not terribly familiar with it, you can always ask for assistance from a mentor, a colleague, or a friend, or even hire someone to help you with the process.

DRAWER 1: RESUMÉ/CV AND PROFESSIONAL PHILOSOPHY

The first drawer of the filing cabinet contains your resumé, CV, and professional philosophy.

RESUMÉ/CV

At the very least, your portfolio should include an updated resumé and/or CV. Remember, these are different from a portfolio in that they present the facts of your career without a corresponding narrative. For more information about these, see Chapter 1.

PROFESSIONAL PHILOSOPHY

Your portfolio should convey your professional philosophy. This should be presented in a narrative format, with an introduction, a body, and a conclusion.

If you aren't sure what your professional philosophy is, try answering the following questions:

- What is your current goal/objective and how do you plan to achieve it?

- What guides your practice as you define it?

- Why do you do what you do, and why is it important and/or impactful?

- What are your core beliefs and values, and how do they guide you?

- What motivates you?

- What have you accomplished thus far in your career?

- What do you still want to accomplish in your career, and how will you do so?

It may be the case that your professional philosophy has changed over the years. This likely reflects growth in your thinking about where you have fit into the nursing profession at different points on your career journey. If you have earlier versions of your professional philosophy written down, include these in your portfolio, too. (You can see one iteration of my personal philosophy in Appendix E.)

DRAWER 2: ACADEMIC EDUCATION, CONTINUING PROFESSIONAL DEVELOPMENT, AND LICENSES AND CERTIFICATIONS

The next drawer of your filing cabinet contains information about your academic education, professional development, and any licenses or certifications you have held during your career.

ACADEMIC EDUCATION

A section outlining your academic education should appear in your portfolio. This should contain copies of diplomas from every institution from which you have received a degree. It is also important to include copies of your transcripts indicating all the coursework and credits you completed in your academic endeavors.

You should list all academic institutions you have attended in this section, even if you did not receive a degree from that institution. You should also include all academic papers—or at least examples—written while at each educational institution. These can serve as the basis or foundation for future efforts in your professional career (Hannans & Olivo, 2017; Sinclair et al., 2013).

CONTINUING PROFESSIONAL DEVELOPMENT

In this section, you want to list any continuing education—both in nursing and *not* in nursing—that you have completed. This will help give the reader a complete picture of you as a professional. This list should include all courses and seminars that you have attended outside of your formal academic education. For each course or seminar, provide the following:

- Whether you attended in person, online, virtually, or some combination of these (if you attended in person, also include the city and state where the course/seminar took place)

- The name of the course or seminar

- The organizing body

- The dates you attended

- A brief description of the course or seminar (their names can be misleading or fail to adequately describe the content presented)

- The number of credits awarded

- A copy of the continuing professional development/continuing nursing education certificate (this can be a paper copy; alternatively, you can provide a link to an electronic version of each certificate)

It's a good idea to maintain an Excel spreadsheet or similar electronic document of all the courses and seminars you have attended, with all this information. Be sure to update it each time you attend a course or seminar! Figure 2.2 shows an example of a blank spreadsheet you could use for this purpose.

	Start / End Date	date	date	0.00	0.00	0.00
Completed Nurse CE Activities			Total		Total	Total
			0.00		0.00	0.00

Activity Title	Date	Credits	Credit Type	Prof	Ethical

0.00	0.00			
Total	Total			
0.00	0.00			

NEA-BC	NPD	Activity - Location	Core Competencies	Provider

FIGURE 2.2 A blank spreadsheet for listing courses, seminars, and such for inclusion in your portfolio.

This section should list all your professional state licenses and include the following information about each one:

- The state in which the license was issued

- Whether that state is a member of the Nurse Licensure Compact

- The license number

- The dates of issuance and expiration

You should also list other licenses that you have obtained in your career but have since expired. For example, if you were once a paramedic but after becoming a registered nurse you let your paramedic license expire, you should still list your paramedic license in this section to show how your career has progressed.

This section should also include any certifications and credentials you have earned. These can be professional or technical in nature. Examples of certifications are Advanced Life Support (ACLS) and Pediatric Advanced Life Support (PALS) Instructor. Examples of credentials are Certified Oncology Nurse (OCN) or Critical Care Registered Nurse (CCRN). You can include in your portfolio a paper copy of each certification or credential or a link to an electronic version. Be sure to document the purpose, issuing authority, and date you received each certificate or credential.

DRAWER 3: EMPLOYMENT HISTORY

In drawer 3 in your filing cabinet is information about your employment history, including any courses you may have taught (if applicable).

This section of your portfolio should provide a narrative of your employment history rather than the list of facts that appears in your resumé or CV. You can divide this section into two sections: one for nursing-related work and another for non-nursing employment. If you are still a student and you have completed a paid internship, assistant-ship, or work-study, you can include this here, too.

For each employment position, list the following information to provide depth and context for your employment history:

- The name of your employer, agency, or organization

- Contact information

- Dates of employment

- Position held

- Offer letter

- Job description and responsibilities

- Salary information (including how your salary progressed throughout your tenure at the organization)

- Evaluations

- Testimonials from patients (without identifying informa-tion), colleagues, clients, and so on (if appropriate)

> **Tip**
>
> If the name of the employer has changed, include its name when you worked there and its updated name.

If your job responsibilities for any position involved teaching certifica-tion or credentialing courses, in-ser-vice courses, and so on, you should include the following information about each one in this section of your portfolio:

> **Tip**
>
> If you held more than one po-sition or title within the same organization, include separate documentation for each one.

- The course name

- Accrediting paperwork

- A copy of the course curriculum

- A copy of any presentations you gave while teaching the course

- The number of course participants

- Course evaluations (or a summary of them) received from course participants

For those of you who have been employed as an academic in a college or university setting, your portfolio should also include information about courses you have coordinated or taught, including:

- The course name

- A copy of the syllabus

- The intended audience

- The number of students

- Course evaluations (or a summary of them) received from students

- Assessments and evaluations from peer reviews of your teaching (if possible)

DRAWER 4: PROFESSIONAL ORGANIZATIONS

Your fourth file cabinet drawer contains information about your commitment to your profession through your involvement in professional organizations. As with the "Employment History" section, this section can be separated into two parts: those professional organizations that pertain to nursing and those that don't.

For each organization, include the following information:

- A copy of your membership card or certificates, in paper format or via link

- Dates of membership

- A brief description of the purpose of the organization

- Any offices held (including the title, the dates or term you were in office, whether the office was elected or appointed, the roles and responsibilities of the office, and any accomplishments or benchmarks you achieved)

- Any committees you chaired (including documentation to describe committee work, with examples)

- Any certificates, commendations, or awards you received from the organization

DRAWER 5: PRESENTATIONS AND PUBLICATIONS

In the fifth file cabinet drawer are items that relate to the dissemination of your knowledge and expertise to provide evidence of your contributions to the profession: presentations and publications.

PRESENTATIONS

In addition to separating this section into two parts—nursing-related presentations and presentations about other topics—it can also include both formal and informal presentations.

Note

This drawer could also note other ways you have disseminated your expertise, such as hosting or contributing to a podcast (e.g., being interviewed on the SigmaCast podcast), keeping a blog, or writing a short piece on a professional organization's website or newsletter (such as Sigma's "Nursing Centered" newsletter).

For each presentation in this section, assemble the following information:

- The presentation title

- The name of the organization or conference where you delivered the presentation

- The date on which you delivered the presentation

- Whether you were invited to deliver it, it was a special session at a conference, or it was accepted as a peer-reviewed abstract

- A hard copy or link of the acceptance letter you received from the organization or conference before you delivered your presentation

- The location where you delivered the presentation (if you delivered it virtually, simply note that, and provide a link to it if possible)

- Whether it was a podium presentation, an oral presentation, a panel discussion, a virtual presentation, or a poster presentation

- The number of participants or attendees (if possible)

- Any evaluations you received regarding the presentation

- A hard copy of or link to your abstract, title page, and any handouts you might have provided for your audience

- If you delivered the presentation at a conference, provide a hard copy or link to the conference brochure and conference proceedings

- A hard copy of any letter or certificate you received from the organization or conference after your presentation

- A link to your abstract in the organization's online library (if it is posted there)

Note

Different organizations might have different terminology for each of these types of presentations. You should use consistent terminology throughout your portfolio. But if you are targeting your portfolio to a specific organization, you should employ that organization's language.

PUBLICATIONS

Again, you can divide this section into two parts: publications that pertain to nursing and publications that don't. Publications include original work that you have authored by yourself or in collaboration with others. You'll want to provide the following information about each publication:

- The manuscript or actual published work

- Whether your work was accepted by a major publication and, if so, the name of that publication

- The letter you received when your work was accepted by a publication (if applicable) or any feedback you received in the event it was rejected

- Whether the manuscript was subject to a peer-review process

Tip

Include *all* your publications in your portfolio. This will show how extensively your work has been disseminated, which is an important part of your career history. Whether your work appeared in a major publication or a less prominent journal, book, monograph, white paper, integrative review, column, social media site, blog, or website, this is an accomplishment, and you should include it.

DRAWER 6: HONORS, AWARDS, SCHOLARSHIPS, AND FELLOWSHIPS

Drawer 6 of your portfolio filing cabinet drawer contains information about any honors and awards you have received or been nominated for during your professional career. It's also where you note any scholarships or fellowships you have earned. These honors, awards, scholarships, and fellowships could relate to nursing or to some other area.

HONORS AND AWARDS

If you have received or been nominated for any honors or awards during your career, cover them in this section. Even if you have received only one honor or award, you should still include it in your career portfolio, as it helps shed light on your entire professional history.

Don't just list your honors and/or awards, like you did in your resumé or CV. The idea here is to provide context as to the nature of each honor or award and why you received it. Specifically, you should include the following for each honor or award:

- The name of the honor or award

- The organization or agency that bestowed the honor or award upon you

- The date you received it

- How frequently the honor or award is given out (annually, biannually, monthly, etc.)

- What the honor or award is given for or represents

- Notable past winners

- Letters you received or other information about the nomination process

- Testimonials or letters of support submitted on your behalf

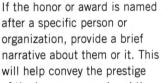

Tip

If the honor or award is named after a specific person or organization, provide a brief narrative about them or it. This will help convey the prestige of the honor or award and the significance of you receiving it.

- A copy or photograph of the certificate or physical award (if applicable)

- Photographs or a recording of the award ceremony (if applicable)

Complete this section by providing evidence of why you received each distinction. This should include a narrative of your body of work or the accomplishments for which you were honored.

> **Tip**
> If you gave an acceptance speech at the award ceremony, include it in your portfolio. If you spoke extemporaneously, jot down some notes about what you said for placement in your portfolio.

SCHOLARSHIPS AND FELLOWSHIPS

You can either include any scholarships and fellowships you have received in the "Honors and Awards" section of your portfolio or present them under a separate heading. Either way, you'll want to provide the same basic type of information about each scholarship and fellowship as you did for each honor and award, plus the amount of each monetary award and the number of years you received it.

> **Tip**
> If you're not sure whether you should include your scholarships and fellowships in the "Honors and Awards" section of your portfolio or present them separately, a good rule of thumb is to use the same approach you used in your resumé or CV.

DRAWER 7: RESEARCH AND GRANTS

The seventh cabinet drawer in your portfolio file cabinet is dedicated to research and scholarship.

RESEARCH

This section of your portfolio provides the reader with information related to any research studies or projects in which you have been involved, where you were not the subject. The idea here is to describe each research study or project and its purpose, including the following information:

- The type of study or project

- Your role in the study or project—for example, primary investigator, team member, research assistant, statistician, and so on

- Whether the study or project is completed or is currently in progress and any relevant dates (such as your start date and your end date, if applicable)

Tip

Do not omit any research study or project from your portfolio because you think your role was insignificant. Every contribution you make is significant, no matter how small!

Note

You'll discuss grant funding in more detail in the next section of your portfolio.

- Whether you received funding for the study or project and, if so, who provided the funding, the dates of the funding period, and the amount of funding you received

You should also indicate whether you published findings from your study or project. If so, you'll want to document the following information for each publication:

- The title of your manuscript

- The length of your manuscript (in pages)

- The name of the publication

- The type of publication (journal, conference proceedings, online resource, and so on)

- The volume (if it was published in a print resource)

- The DOI number and link (if it was published in an online resource)

- The date of publication

- The names and credentials of any co-authors (if applicable)

If you have published Doctor of Nursing Practice projects, evidence-based projects, integrative or narrative reviews, quality-improvement projects, or similar, be sure to include these in this section of your portfolio. Don't leave your work out! If you like, you can use a more specific section header for these, such as "Scholar-ship" or "Evidence-Based Projects."

> **Tip**
> If your findings were disseminated in more than one publication, you should document each one.

GRANTS

Use this section of your portfolio to provide information about grants you have received as an individual, as a member of a team, and/or in a career role—for example, a Health Resources and Services Administration grant for student funding in an academic institution.

For each grant you have been awarded, include the following information:

- The name of the grant

- The name of the granting agency

- The amount of the grant

- The purpose of the grant

- The duration of the grant (with dates)

- An executive summary of the grant

- A print or electronic copy of your grant application

- A print or electronic copy of your acceptance letter

- Paperwork or other information that relates to any additional funding you received (if applicable)

DRAWER 8: COMMITTEE WORK, MILITARY SERVICE, AND COMMUNITY SERVICE

The eighth file cabinet drawer should cover any community service you've completed, including committee work and military service.

COMMITTEE WORK

Being an active member of committees—including employment committees, committees for professional and non-professional organizations, nursing and non-nursing committees, and any other type of committee of which you are a member—provides evidence of your commitment to your community, colleagues, and the nursing profession as a whole. While your committee work might seem not as important as other items in your portfolio, many prospective employers will be extremely interested in your level of engagement in this type of work.

For each committee on which you have served, include the following information:

- A brief description of the committee and its purpose

- Your role on the committee

- How often the committee meets and by which method (in person, virtually, or some combination of the two)

- Examples of the work you have done or projects you have completed, including paper copies or links to online materials (if applicable)

MILITARY SERVICE

For many nursing professionals, the military was their first employer—especially those who served in the Reserve Officer Training Corps. Still, for various reasons, many nursing professionals omit their military service from career-related documents, including their portfolio.

This is a mistake. Your military history is of great interest to potential employers. Not only do members of the military provide a great service to the country, they also receive valuable leadership opportunities, are accustomed to maintaining confidentiality, and are held to high legal and ethical standards. These attributes are important in healthcare, nursing theory, emergent situations, and so much more! So, you should always include your military history (if applicable) in your portfolio. It might be what sets you apart from others!

Specifically, you should include the following information:

- Your branch of service

- Your dates of service from entry to discharge

- Your rank progression

- The type of discharge you received

- Copies of your enlistment, promotion, and discharge papers

- Copies of commendations you have received

- Reviews and evaluations

- Whether you are still in the reserves

> *Note*
> Never minimize your military service in your career portfolio.

> *Tip*
> Because of the potential sensitivity of any of this information, maintain confidentiality relating to yourself and others as appropriate.

COMMUNITY SERVICE

It is essential to include a record of community-service activities in your portfolio. This can often differentiate you from other applicants for a position. For example, suppose you are applying for a new position in oncology. If you've participated in community-service activities to raise money or provide services to support programs associated with cancer causes, you should include this in your portfolio and highlight it during your interview.

Although you might not have evidentiary materials for every community-service project you have participated in, you should maintain as complete a list of these activities as possible. This list should include the following information about each community-service activity you've done:

- The name of the community-service organization you worked with

- A description of the type of activity you did

- Your role in the activity

- The date(s) of the activity

If you do have evidentiary materials for any of these activities or the service organizations involved—in paper or electronic form—you should absolutely include them with your portfolio. For example, maybe you received a certificate or commendation upon completion of the activity. Or maybe you have photos or a video of the activity taking place. If so, you should include them. You might also include letters on your behalf from leaders of the service organization or testimonials from others. You can also extrapolate documentation for more recent activities to activities in the past for which you might not have the same type of evidence.

Tip

Even if you don't have access to evidentiary materials for community-service activities you've done in the past, you should start collecting these types of materials when you engage in community-service activities from here on out!

DRAWER 9: MISCELLANEOUS

The ninth and final file cabinet drawer of your portfolio can be labelled "Miscellaneous." This drawer should contain items that do not fit neatly into any of the other sections mentioned so far. For example, I put information about my nursing consultation business in this section of my portfolio. A reflective summary statement can also be placed here.

NURSING CONSULTATION

You might engage in nursing consultation as part of your broader employment responsibilities or as a career position in and of itself. This will factor into how you shape this section.

Either way, you should begin this section with a statement on how you define consulting for you and your work. If someone who wants to hire you as an independent consultant requests to see your portfolio, you want to be sure they understand what you bring to the table, and this definition will help clarify this. If you are consulting as part of your employment responsibilities for an organization, you should also provide a brief description of how your consulting work fits into your overall job or position.

If you are an independent nursing consultant, you'll want to include information about each consultative position you have held, including the following:

- The company or organization you consulted for

- The start and end dates

- Whether you were paid for your services or you offered them on a volunteer basis

- A description of the project you worked on and the major outcomes you achieved

- Paper or electronic copies of letters of agreement or hire

- Correspondence that evaluates your work, thanks you for it, or serves as a testimonial

- Whether you were asked to do follow-up projects or new projects for the same company or organization

Note

Assuming you can maintain confidentiality, you can use your portfolio to provide examples of your work, from proposals to executive summaries to completed work products.

REFLECTIVE OR SUMMARY STATEMENT

You can include a reflective or summary statement in the "Miscella-neous" section of your portfolio or place it in its own section if you pre-fer. This statement requires you to look back at your career and think about what you have accomplished, what you still want to do, and how you think you might do it, taking your professional philosophy into account.

As you write your reflective statement, do the following:

- Reflect on your accomplishments.

- Focus on both your strengths and your weaknesses as a professional nurse.

- Provide both positive and negative assessments of your work.

- Describe challenging situations and how you handled them.

- Discuss struggles you've had during your career and how you overcame them.

- Describe lessons learned and how you addressed them.

- Give examples of how you affected particular patients or families and how they affected you.

- Consider how you have affected the diverse individuals and groups you have worked with during your career.

- Consider how you have made a difference in the world in which you practice.

Tip

It is often difficult for professionals to reflect on their careers. Writing about yourself and your career can be daunting. To help with this, consider writing an outline or jotting down notes in a journal that you can build from instead of starting your narrative from scratch.

MISCELLANEOUS

This can include documents or other materials that are part of your career history but do not fit neatly into the other sections of your portfolio. For example, you might store historical data that is not relevant per se but could pertain to your career journey. This could include documents of any type discussed previously that relate to your career history but not your *nursing* career history—especially if you are a second-degree student.

TIME TO START THE PROCESS

Now that you know the importance of developing and maintaining a portfolio to reflect on and advance your career, start collecting all the documents, materials, Post-its, notepads, and other repositories of information about where you have been and what you have done during your professional career. Then find a "storage" system that works best for you—maybe a large binder or an online resource.

Putting your career history all in one "file cabinet" will provide you not only with a means of both organizing and updating your information but also a sense of accomplishment, no matter what point of your career you have reached. It also enables you to quickly and easily apply for new jobs, promotions, grants, and so much more. There is a great sense of relief in knowing that whatever you need to provide to anyone on your career journey, including yourself, is easily obtainable. No more stress, no more delays, no more searching your residence or office for a note you left yourself about a presentation you did last year!

RESOURCES FOR E-PORTFOLIOS

Some nurses present their portfolios in electronic format—in other words, as e-portfolios. This simply means they create a website for their portfolio. The following sites offer resources and information for creating websites for this purpose and are widely used by nursing professionals:

- https://www.wix.com

- https://www.foliotek.com/professional-portfolio

- https://www.squarespace.com/websites/create-a-portfolio/

- https://wordpress.org/

- https://www.weebly.com

- https://portfolio.adobe.com

Note that it is not our intent here to recommend one of these sites over the others. Also note that before you decide on which of these sites (or some other site) you want to use, you must be sure it includes all the features you want and understand any costs associated with using them. Be as thorough as possible when determining if an e-portfolio is something you want to create and what site best meets your needs.

REFERENCES

Green, J., Wyllie, A., & Jackson, D. (2014). Electronic portfolios in nursing education: A review of the literature. *Nurse Education in Practice, 14*(1), 4–8. https://doi.org/10.1016/j.nepr.2013.08.011

Hannans, J., & Olivo, Y. (2017). Craft a positive nursing digital identity with an ePortfolio. *American Nurse Today, 12*(11), 48–49.

Madden, K., Collins, E., & Lander, P. (2019). Nursing students' perspectives on ePortfolios: Themes and preferences compared with paper-based experiences. *International Journal of ePortfolio, 9*(2), 87–96.

Sinclair, P., Bowen, L., & Donkin, C. B. (2013). Professional nephrology nursing portfolios: Maintaining competence to practise. *Renal Society of Australasia Journal, 9*(1), 35–40.

St-Germain, D., Cote, V., Gagnon, C., Laurin, A. C., Bélanger, L., Lambert, A., & Gagné-Sauvé, C. (2019). The INSEPArable research project: A transdisciplinary caring approach to the design of a portfolio for reflexive nursing practices. *International Journal of Caring Sciences, 12*(1), 132–141.

3

YOUR NURSING IDENTITY

With Contributing Author Christina Ferrell, PhD, RN, NEA-BC

"I am often asked, who am I as a nurse? What do I do and how do I define myself in my career? If I am not at the bedside, others outside of nursing often do not understand how I am still a nurse. I can be having a discussion with someone who knows me or someone who does not know me, and both question my 'nursingness.' Who am I if others have such a narrow view of nurses and nursing professionals? How should I describe myself to others? Maybe others do not know who I am or what I do as a nurse because I do not articulate who I am and what I do well enough."

–P. L., DNP, ARNP-BC

"In my early days as a nurse manager, I struggled to maintain a grasp on my value to patient care and nursing. I was no longer wearing a uniform, doing nursing tasks, or applying my critical thinking to direct patient care. My knowledge seemed to have plummeted, and I felt removed from nursing skills. I simply could not sense the contributions I was making. I remember thinking, 'I am working so hard, but I cannot see the results.' As a new leader, I would have benefited greatly from understanding that these were the pains of my nursing professional identity reforming. As I matured, I realized my value was in using my nursing knowledge to ensure that the right policies, practices, and resources were in place for the best possible care to occur. My authentic self's presence was key to showing my commitment to supporting and developing those providing the patient care. My nursing knowledge allowed me to be an advocate and to speak/translate the nursing language to other disciplines. I realized nursing and caring occurs without putting on gloves and a uniform. As the cloud settled, I was able to visualize the nursing I was doing, the value of my nursing knowledge, and the aspects that were me—still being a nurse."

–C. H., RN, MSN

WHAT IS NURSING IDENTITY?

"To every being as such there belongs identity, the unity with itself."

–Martin Heidegger

The first time most of us hear about who we are as nurses is during one of our first courses in nursing school—the one that covers key concepts of professional nursing. In this class, we are taught the definition of the word *nurse*, our responsibilities as a nurse, and how nurses identify themselves—not just by title or name, but by education, experience, our role, and our responsibilities. Indeed, professional identity is a core foundation of the nursing profession (Godfrey & Young, 2020).

Often, the notions of a nursing identity and a nursing image are interchanged. But there are important differences. Our *nursing identity* is our internal view of ourselves and our own personal career expectations. Our *nursing image*, in contrast, is how others describe us and what we do. Not surprisingly, many nurses grapple with these incongruencies.

The preponderance of literature on nursing identity focuses mainly on how nursing students and new graduates develop their sense of self as a nurse. It has only been during the last five to 10 years that the literature has shown an increase in the exploration of professional identity in nurses beyond their early career years. This is important because our professional identity can change and expand as our careers evolve over time. Specifically, our perceptions of ourselves as nursing professionals can be influenced by:

- Our experience

- Our expertise

- Our career position(s)

- Our responsibilities

- With whom we interact, and how, in our diverse roles as a nurse

> **Note**
>
> As nurses, we incorporate the fundamental values and ideals of the nursing profession into our everyday actions. Actions such as practicing with integrity, providing care to others, and leading efforts to improve lives are observable aspects of our individual nursing professional identity.

- Our career advancement and the new behaviors necessary to maintain and grow our careers

The National League for Nursing states that professional identity is "evident in our way of doing, knowing and being" (NLN, 2010, p. 35). Although these terms may sound odd, these are the three areas of concern when nurses consider taking their careers in a new direction. Typically, we are seeking a change in what we are doing as a professional nurse, in the knowledge we can apply, or in the experience of being a nurse in our current role.

NURSES ON NURSING IDENTITY

In an interview-based study conducted by Ferrell (2017), several nurses described their thoughts on their career identity. These comments offer perspective on how career identity can be defined by diverse nurses based on their experiences. Some of these nurses no longer work at the bedside. Because of how the general public defines nursing, these nurses are often asked, "Are you still a nurse?" or "Why don't you practice nursing anymore?"

"I don't know how to be [except to be] a nurse. The way I view the world is through the nurse lens. And what I am is a nurse. I like to say there are 'nurses that are nurses through and through,' or, 'they are a nurse's nurse.' Nursing identity is about looking the part, being good in the part, walking the walk, and talking the talk."

–Participant #1 (p. 91)

"Nursing identity changes from one role to the next. I think it should change. Moving from the student nurse to the practicing nurse, to whatever it is you are going to do in nursing, i.e., chief nursing officer or even chief executive officer, whatever it is, identity does have to change. One must recognize what their identity is or run the risk of not meeting their full potential and meeting the obligations you have to the people that look to you."

–Participant #2 (p. 92)

"Being a nurse is not about the physical but rather the whole core of what nursing is about and what being a nurse is and your self-identity. It is not about the uniforms or physical attributes. I would describe it more as our deep-seated values, and those values drive behaviors. Nurses have a deep core of valuing other people, caring about other people, and being able to translate that into care. I translate that to genuine care of our students, our staff, our faculty, and the organizations and communities that we serve."

–Participant #4 (p. 94)

"When asked, 'What is it that you do?' I think it is not what you do or how you do it, but who are you doing it for. Authenticity of who I am has to be evident in my way of being in the world and in my practice. Who I am is my essence and my comportment."

–Participant #5 (p. 95)

Godfrey and Young (2020) expanded on these NLN attributes to include doing, being, acting ethically, flourishing, and changing identities. Each of these attributes encompasses how nurses see themselves in their roles throughout their careers and how nurses grow and advance their behaviors within the discipline of nursing.

REFLECTING ON YOUR NURSING JOURNEY

Your nursing journey is an ever-evolving path of learning who you are and who you want to be as a nurse. There are countless questions you can ask yourself along that path. Many of those questions simply relate to the practicality of your choice; others go much deeper in search of your vision of meaning, purpose, and success. For example:

- What activities do you consider to be "doing nursing"?

- Do you feel a sense of purpose from these nursing activities?

- Are you able to do nursing to the extent that it brings you pride?

- What caring practices—not skills, but practices—are you able to provide in your role?

- Do you feel your current role affords you the opportunity to care for others?

- How do you use or apply your nursing knowledge?

- Is your nursing knowledge being appropriately utilized?

- Do you desire more knowledge? Is that knowledge formal or informal?

- What aspects of your role allow you to act or feel like a nurse?

- What scenarios bring you the most pride in being a nurse?

- How does being a nurse, having nursing knowledge, and doing nursing enhance your life and the lives of others?

When contemplating these questions, it is best to think in terms of what being a nurse means to you and your own identity. Ultimately, your nursing identity intertwines your personal and professional attributes and knowledge.

> **Note**
> Understanding your nursing identity is helpful in internalizing the nurse you are and the nurse you want to become.

This self-reflection may not be as straightforward as one might think. Some nurses struggle to clearly articulate these thoughts. This might be because the amount of nursing performed in a role does not necessarily correlate to a stronger sense of nursing identity. Nurses in direct care roles may feel like they are constrained from providing the care they envision, are unable to apply their nursing knowledge, or lack fulfillment in being a nurse in that setting. In contrast, nurses in roles that do not involve direct patient care might have a powerful sense of how their work contributes to the care of others, a clear vision for applying their nursing knowledge, and a strong belief that being a nurse in that setting brings them meaning and purpose.

> **Note**
> Your day-to-day experiences of being a nurse help craft your professional nursing identity.

DEFINING YOUR NURSING IDENTITY

In working with nurses at all points in their careers, I've observed that many of them find it difficult to articulate their nursing identity. In particular, they struggle when examining their current state and contemplating where they might want to be in their future.

To assist in this effort, I have created an exercise to define your nursing identity using a schematic. This schematic provides a means to identify what you have accomplished so far, what you are working toward accomplishing in the future, and therefore, how you define your professional identity. For example, suppose you are an academic preparing for promotion, tenure, and reappointment (PTR). In that case, you could base your schematic on the requirements and expectations of that process as it relates to your position.

> *Note*
>
> A nursing identity schematic enables you to visualize how you are building your career based on your perception of yourself as a nursing professional.

Figure 3.1 shows the schematic for an academic who views her nursing identity as a "master educator." In defining her career identity, she included requirements for PTR: teaching, scholarship, and service. She also considered her upcoming evaluation, which would focus on her research and publications. Note that she links all her work to her identity as a master educator, including her clinical practice, teaching students, and mentoring faculty. She also uses those same topical areas to expand and advance her research, publications, and grant applications.

Figure 3.2 shows a similar schematic for a clinical practitioner in a leadership position. This nurse wanted to define his nursing identity and related work, accomplishments, and goals in preparation for an upcoming evaluation. The evaluation, he knew, would be focused on expanding his leadership role to promote and disseminate evidence-based practice projects and on his overall performance as a clinician. So, in defining his career identity, he incorporated the expectations for his position and for his own growth. Note that he links all his work to his identity as a clinical practitioner.

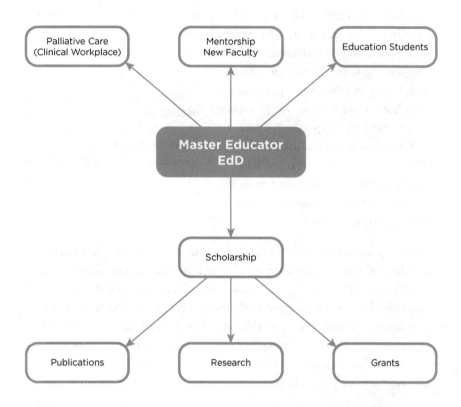

FIGURE 3.1 Defining your nursing identity: master educator.

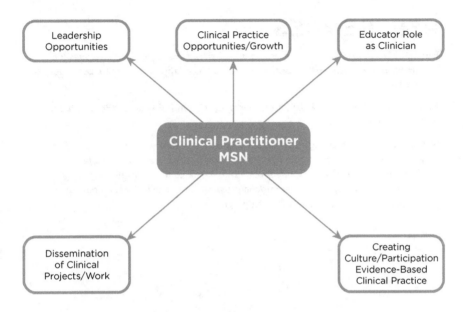

FIGURE 3.2 Defining your nursing identity: clinical practitioner.

Anyone at any point in their career can create this type of career identity schematic. Note, however, that it should be fluid. You and your nursing identity will mature over the continuum of your career. You will form and reform your nursing identity as you expand your capacity to practice and seek fulfillment along your career path. So, your schematic should change along with it. Ultimately, this schematic should serve as an evidentiary document that notes your progress *and* as a map to guide you as you grow and expand your career.

> *Note*
>
> The schematic enables you to frame your nursing identity in a pragmatic and logical manner for yourself and for others, such as a supervisor or other evaluator (when applicable). For help creating your own schematic, see Appendix F.

REFERENCES

Ferrell, C. D. (2017). *Nursing professional identity: The experiences and meanings for nursing in senior leadership positions* [Doctoral dissertation]. ProQuest Dissertations and Theses.

Godfrey, N., & Young, E. (2020). Professional identity. In J. F. Giddens (Ed.), *Concepts of nursing practice* (3rd ed.). Elsevier Publishing.

National League for Nursing. (2010). *Outcomes and competencies for graduates of practical/vocational, diploma, associate degree, baccalaureate degree, master's practice, doctorate and research doctorate programs in nursing.* http://www.nln.org/professional-development-programs/competencies-for-nursing-education/nln-competencies-for-graduates-of-nursing-programs

4

EDUCATIONAL ADVANCEMENT: GAINING NEW EXPERTISE

"I have been a nurse for over 20 years. I have been in different positions in the clinical organization where I have worked since I graduated from nursing school. I love what I do, but I start thinking there is more out there for me to do and learn every time I am at a conference or read a journal article. But am I too old to be thinking about another degree? How would I do this when I am not tech-savvy? How would I pay for this? Am I making excuses and putting up roadblocks? If I do not pursue my education now, maybe I never will. I need advice. How do I figure this all out, and who will help me?

–K. G., BSN, CCRN

"I finally have realized that I want to keep going to school and advancing my education. This will open more professional doors for me. I am not sure what direction I should go in and what programs will be best to meet my desire to go further in nursing. I think I want to get a doctoral degree because everyone keeps telling me that this is the future, but how do I know if that is right for me? I have only been a nurse for a short time, so how do I know what I will want to be doing in my future?"

–A. F., BSN, RN

KNOW THYSELF: DECIDING IF FURTHER EDUCATION IS RIGHT FOR YOU

Determining whether an advanced educational path is the right one for you can be daunting, confusing, and overwhelming. Indeed, for many nurses, especially more seasoned ones, the thought of going back to school can be downright scary. One side of your brain tells you that this is your time. It's your chance to learn and grow and move forward in your career! But the other side questions whether you can take on an educational challenge in addition to your full-time job and your responsibilities to family or friends.

If you're considering going back to school, you might be asking yourself some of these questions:

- Am I ready to go back to school at this point in my life?

- Now that I have career security and have developed a certain level of expertise at work, do I really want to start over?

- How would I manage going back to school personally, physically, and financially?

- I am so new in my career; do I really want to go back to school already?

- Why is everyone pushing me to go back to school?

You should not return to school for any length of time without thinking things through. There are several factors to consider, many of which are inextricably linked:

- What do you want to do next in your career and as you advance farther along your career path?

- Is this the best time for you to return to school?

- What type of educational program matches your career ambitions?

- What type of educational program do you want to pursue?

- Where do you want to pursue your education?

- Do you have geographical mobility?

- Do you have the financial means to pay for your education, or will you need to seek alternative sources of funding?

- Will you be able to balance and manage your personal, professional, and academic responsibilities?

- Are you interested in an online or virtual program, a face-to-face program, or a combination (hybrid) of the two?

- Are you interested in a full-time or part-time program?

- Do you want to pursue a particular area of focus, concentration, or research?

- Are there specific faculty members with whom you want to work?

When making this decision, take your time, reflect on your career, and put in the work to determine if this move is right for you. Oh, and remember to *breathe*!

ABCS OF ADVANCING YOUR EDUCATION

A   Assessment of self

B   Belief in self

C   Commitment and confidence

D   Desire, determination, and drive

E   Exploration and endurance

F   Fortitude and fervor

YOU'VE DECIDED . . . NOW WHAT?

After much soul-searching, you have decided you are ready to continue your education. So, what should you do next? Here are the steps you should take:

1. Decide what degree to pursue.

2. Do your research.

3. Explore program offerings.

4. Narrow down your options.

5. "Interview" the program.

6. Complete the application process.

7. Choose your program.

The following sections describe each of these steps in detail.

Tip

The internet is a great place to find information about advancing your nursing career. You can start at these sites: Sigma Theta Tau International (https://www.sigmanursing.org), the National League for Nursing (NLN; http://www.nln.org), and the American Association of Colleges of Nursing (AACN; https://www.aacnnursing.org).

STEP 1: DECIDING WHAT DEGREE TO PURSUE

Chances are you have a general idea what you want to do next on your career journey, but you are not sure what degree will help you get there or provide you with the most options now and in the future. Thus, your first step is to determine what degree to pursue. Fortunately, one of the best things about professional nursing is the diverse and varied opportunities for advancement through education. No matter where you are in your career journey, you can partake in numerous educational programs that will enhance your experience and advance your career.

To decide what type of degree you should pursue, ask yourself:

- What area of nursing do you want to study?

- Are you interested in practice, education, administration, or health policy?

- Do you want to use evidence-based practice at the bedside?

- Do you want to be a primary care practitioner?

- Do you want to move into a clinical nurse leader role?

- Do you want to be an educator or clinical instructor?

- Does the political arena interest you?

- Do you want to combine your nursing degree with a law or business degree?

Also consider the availability of various positions in the area of nursing you want to study, their salaries, the overall work environment, and opportunities for continued advancement and collaborations.

Here are a few areas you might consider if you are interested in pursuing an advanced degree:

- Nurse practitioner

- Nurse educator

- Nurse administrator

- Clinical nurse specialist

- Clinical nurse leader

You can also opt to advance your education even further by obtaining a terminal degree in any number of nursing-related disciplines. A *terminal degree* is defined as the highest degree given in a particular field of study.

> **Tip**
> Sometimes it helps to identify what types of advancement opportunities are available in your organization, determine what the educational requirements are, and work from there.

CAREER BYTE: HELPFUL TERMINOLOGY

Here's a list of terms that may help you in your attempt to determine which degree program is right for you:

- **RN to BSN:** A completion program—usually lasting one year—for the ADN graduate.

- **Graduate entry:** A program that grants a master of science in nursing (MSN) or master of nursing (MN) degree in a seamless curriculum. This is usually a two- to three-year program. Some programs grant the BSN at the completion of the requisite education; others subsume the BSN education into the master's degree program. Upon completion of the baccalaureate component of this program, as defined by the college/university and the state board of nursing, the individual will be eligible to sit for the NCLEX-RN examination.

- **Master of science in nursing (MSN):** This type of program might be focused on advanced practices, such as preparing individuals as nurse practitioners, clinical nurse specialists, nurse midwives, or nurse anesthetists. Alternatively, it might have a nursing education or administration focus, both with advanced clinical practice foundations. This is usually a one- to two-year program.

- **Master of nursing (MN):** The same as an MSN degree. (Different colleges and universities use different lettering for similar degrees.)

- **Clinical nurse leader (CNL):** An accelerated program in which nurses are prepared at an advanced level to remain at the bedside using an evidence-based nursing framework. This is not considered an advanced practice degree because preparation occurs at a generalist level rather than a specialist level.

- **Clinical nurse specialist (CNS):** A clinical nurse specialist is an advanced practice registered nurse who holds a graduate degree in nursing—master's or doctorate. A CNS is an expert clinician in a specialized area of nursing practice in diverse healthcare settings. The CNS can manage patients as well as provide support and resources for nurses at the bedside. A CNS is a leader in developing and promoting practice changes in a healthcare organization.

- **Doctor of philosophy (PhD):** A research-based terminal degree. A PhD prepares students for research and academic positions.

- **Doctor of nursing science (DNS or DNSc):** Equivalent to a PhD. (Again, different colleges and universities use different lettering for similar degrees.)

- **Doctor of science in nursing (DSN):** Equivalent to a PhD. (Again, different colleges and universities use different lettering for similar degrees.)

- **Doctor of nursing practice (DNP):** An advanced-level clinical terminal degree without the research emphasis of a PhD or a similar terminal research degree. A DNP prepares students for leadership positions in all areas of clinical practice including (but not limited to) patient care, health policy implementation and evaluation, and evidence-based nursing research.

- **Doctor of nursing practice (DrNP):** Equivalent to a DNP. (Again, different colleges and universities use different lettering for similar degrees.)

- **Doctor of education (EdD):** A non–research focused terminal degree with a focus on teaching, including development, implementation, and evaluation of teaching strategies and methods.

NURSE PRACTITIONER

Nurse practitioners can work and lead in diverse settings beyond primary care. If serving as a nurse practitioner in primary care is of interest to you, now would be a perfect time to work toward that goal. As we as a nation and society emerge from the COVID-19 pandemic, the need for nurse practitioners will continue to grow. The general public's trust in nurses is the highest among all professionals—meaning that the number of individuals and families seeking care from nurse practitioners is likely to climb. Nurse practitioners will continue to be on the front lines, working with clients in clinics, pharmacies, and other nontraditional primary care settings. At the same time, we might soon face a nursing shortage at all levels due to post-traumatic stress disorder and/or burnout in the aftermath of the pandemic.

If you are considering becoming a nurse practitioner, you must complete an advanced graduate degree in nursing—that is, a clinical master's degree or a doctor of nursing practice degree. Be aware, however, that entry-level educational requirements for nurse practitioners will likely change in the future. In 2015, the AACN declared that entry-level educational requirements for nurse practitioners should be a DNP degree (although as of 2021, this has not come to pass). Similarly, in 2018, the National Organization of Nurse Practitioner Faculties committed to moving all entry-level nurse practitioner education to the DNP level by 2025. On a related note, some states have phased out master's programs for advanced practice, but most states still allow advanced practice education to be at the master's level. And some specialty areas require a DNP—for example, nurse anesthesia and nurse midwifery—but this is not currently enforced. All this is to say that if this is your chosen path, you will want to keep up to date on this issue.

NURSE EDUCATOR

If you are interested in nursing education, an advanced degree—such as an MSN, MN, PhD, or EdD—is certainly helpful. However, depending on what type of teaching you want to do, it might not be necessary. For example, suppose you want to work as a preceptor in your clinical organization. In that case, you might simply want to participate in preceptorship classes offered at a nearby school or college of nursing or at your clinical agency. In addition, some community colleges or schools of nursing hire baccalaureate-prepared nurses to teach clinicals for undergraduate students, so you could pursue those opportunities as well. Four-year colleges or schools of nursing generally require at least a master's degree, even to teach clinicals. On a related note, if you do want to pursue a degree in this area, you can talk to schools and colleges of nursing in your area about what opportunities might be available for teaching assistantships to help finance your continued education.

NURSE ADMINISTRATOR

Nursing administration offers many possibilities in diverse clinical settings. As with nurse education positions, having an advanced degree, such as an MSN, MN, MSN-MBA, CNS, or PhD, can help you obtain a position as a nurse administrator but might not be strictly required. Instead, you might consider seeking out continuing education courses that relate to administration. This will not only prepare you to take on a nurse administrator role but also help you evaluate whether you like the job enough to pursue it further by obtaining an advanced degree. (The same goes for talking to colleagues or mentors who are nurse administrators.)

> **Tip**
>
> Check out additional professional education courses through the American Organization for Nursing Leadership (AONL), formerly the American Organization for Nurse Executives, at https://www.aonl.org/education/overview.

CLINICAL NURSE SPECIALIST OR CLINICAL NURSE LEADER

Those of you who have an interest in leadership across health disciplines for individuals and groups of clients in diverse settings might want to consider either of the following master's degree programs:

- **Clinical nurse specialist (CNS):** A CNS is an expert in evidence-based nursing and practice in varied settings and with diverse populations. A CNS provides direct patient care. In addition, a CNS might engage in such varied activities as teaching, mentoring, management, research, consulting, and systems improvement (AACN, 2006). With their depth and breadth of expertise, a CNS can work with healthcare professionals across settings, ensuring the provision of high-quality care to patients, families, groups, and communities. A CNS degree is considered an advanced practice degree.

- **Clinical nurse leader (CNL):** A CNL is prepared to be a leader in all healthcare-delivery settings. A CNL does not have one specific role; rather, this person is accountable for the delivery of evidence-based nursing care, client outcomes, and coordination of the healthcare team. If you have broad interest in the provision of healthcare for small front-line units or microsystems, this is a role you might want to consider. Unlike a CNS, who is educated as a specialist, a CNL is educated as a generalist. Therefore, the CNL is not considered an advanced practice degree.

OBTAINING A TERMINAL DEGREE

You can pursue a terminal degree in various disciplines, such as nursing, higher education, public policy, anthropology, and the social sciences, among many others. As mentioned, a *terminal degree* is defined as the highest degree given in a particular field of study. Usually this is a doctoral degree but not always. In some fields, a master's degree is considered a terminal degree. An example is a master of fine arts for a field such as studio architecture. You might seek this degree if you want to combine your nursing experience with architecture to build more efficient healthcare facilities.

There are several types of terminal degrees. The most common of these is a doctor of philosophy (PhD). The PhD is considered the terminal degree for many academic and research fields in most countries. (Universities in the United Kingdom offer higher doctoral degrees, such as the doctor of sciences.) In some countries, a master's degree is considered the terminal degree, so if you plan to attend school outside of North America, be sure to inquire about what degree that country considers to be terminal.

In addition to the PhD, nurses interested in earning a terminal degree that pertains to the nursing profession can obtain one (or more) of the following:

- Doctor of nursing science (DNS or DNSc)

- Doctor of science in nursing (DSN)

- Doctor of nursing practice (DNP or DrNP)

> **Tip**
>
> Refer to the sidebar "Career Byte: Helpful Terminology" earlier in this chapter for more information on these types of terminal degrees.

A doctor of education degree (EdD) is yet another terminal degree available to nurses. A nurse might earn this degree if they want to become a nurse educator at a college or university.

When considering a nursing-related doctoral degree, you often enter a confusing arena. According to the AACN, most new doctoral programs in nursing have led to a PhD degree in nursing, which continues to be the traditional doctoral degree in nursing. In addition, many existing DNS, DNSc, and DSN programs have been converted to PhD in nursing programs. But arguments have been made in the past for and against distinguishing the PhD from the DNS or DNSc and similar nursing degrees; today, these degrees are widely seen as being equal. In fact, the AACN (2001, p. 2) recommends "continuing with a single set of quality indicators for research-focused doctoral programs in nursing whether the program leads to a PhD or a DNS degree." While some schools still make slight coursework distinctions between the PhD and DSN degrees, the attainment of a PhD, DNS, DNSc, or DSN degree is viewed as preparatory for both academic and research positions.

> **Tip**
>
> The type of degree you choose often depends on whether you want more emphasis on academic or teaching coursework or research coursework.

There is also a debate that pits the PhD against the DNP (or DrNP). This debate relates more broadly to which degree is suited for a particular focus and whether the educational requirements for each degree are comparable so they can be preparatory in similar settings. In theory, a PhD is a research-focused terminal degree, while a DNP is a clinical-based terminal degree. In practice, however, more emphasis is placed on the fact that both degrees are terminal degrees and are thus equal in terms of educational preparation. Of course, this is not true. The curricula for both degrees are distinct. Moreover, this thinking does a disservice to the person who holds the degree, imposing on them expectations that they might not have been prepared for and often leading to dissatisfaction in their role. To attempt to address this issue, some learning institutions have developed combination PhD-DNP programs as well as bridge programs from PhD to DNP and vice versa. These types of programs broaden your education and prepare you for both a research and/or academic role and an advanced clinical role.

You're probably wondering how to figure out what terminal degree is best for you. Here are a few points to consider:

- If you're interested in teaching nursing in a university school or college of nursing, consider a PhD in nursing education or higher education. If your long-term goal is to become the dean or director of a nursing program at a university or college, you could specialize in an area such as higher education administration. Or, if your interest is in academics, you might specialize in curriculum, instruction, and/or evaluation.

> **Note**
>
> Some programs grant an EdD for those interested in education without the more heavily emphasized research focus of a PhD.

- If you want to conduct nursing research, study translational or implementation science, teach at a research academic setting, and/or work with a governmental or funding agency conducting scientific research, consider pursuing a PhD in nursing, a DNS, or a DNSc. You can also consider a PhD in another related area, such as higher education, sociology, anthropology, healthcare administration, or an interdisciplinary PhD. This type of degree can be useful for those who want to conduct research for the National Institutes of Health or the National Institute of Nursing Research, or who want to conduct research at a university while also pursuing the role of nurse educator.

- If your goal is to work in a clinical environment, making change in healthcare systems, then the DNP is for you. If teaching is also of interest to you, you can take some education coursework separately from the DNP. (Note that if you are *especially* interested in teaching—more than in the clinical aspects of your job—the DNP degree might not be for you.)

BECOMING A HEALTHCARE POLICYMAKER

Recently, more and more nurses have become interested in healthcare policy issues. This is no doubt because healthcare is now at the forefront of the political arena, thanks to issues such as COVID-19, equity in healthcare, and healthcare costs, among others.

Nurses can make a profound difference by participating in the development of healthcare policy. One way to do this is to explore possible internships with local or state politicians and political action groups. If you have mobility, you could even explore internships or volunteering opportunities in Washington, DC, with political lobbying groups and your state representative and senator.

Nurses who are interested in being even more involved in healthcare policy should consider seeking a master's degree or a doctoral degree in this area. Healthcare policy, similar to public health, can be part of a comprehensive nursing curriculum or pursued as a primary focused degree. If you go that route, it's a good idea to seek out a part-time position with a think tank or healthcare agency that might be willing to financially support efforts to advance your education.

If you are unsure about an advanced degree in healthcare policy, consider a fellowship—for example through the Robert Wood Johnson Foundation (https://www.healthpolicyfellows.org/), through a university, or through a governmental agency.

You can also pursue an interdisciplinary doctoral degree. That is, with
the assistance of a faculty advisor,
you can create a doctoral program
that meets your more specific needs
or interests, such as in public health,
nursing, or sociology.

> **Tip**
> As you consider which ad-
> vanced or terminal degree is
> right for you, think about what
> you want to get out of the
> degree rather than the degree's
> letters. Often, different colleges
> and universities use different
> lettering for similar degrees.

STEP 2: DOING YOUR RESEARCH

Once you have a general idea of what type of degree you want to
pursue, you can begin doing your research. This step is especially important. It's critical to learn as much as you can about the degree, the
positions available for someone who earns the degree, and the institutions that grant the degree.

Begin your research by talking to colleagues, peers, role models, mentors, and other people whose opinions you value about the degree that
interests you. Specifically, ask them:

- Do they think the degree is a good fit for you?

- Do they know anyone else who has pursued the same degree?

- Do they have insight into which educational institutions offer
  strong programs for the degree?

It's also a good idea to peruse professional journals in the area of study
you want to pursue. Who is writing professional or research-based
articles in your area of interest? What colleges or universities do they
represent? This might help you narrow down—or in some cases, broad-
en—your search.

Beyond that, you can use online resources to assist you in your research:

- If you want to know more about a particular degree or area of
  study, begin by researching those. For example, to view white

papers on various degree programs, visit the AACN website (https://www.aacnnursing.org). To see a list of accredited programs offering both BSN and MSN degrees, see the NLN website (http://www.nln.org). Both these sites also provide information about various degree options, doctoral program options, employment opportunities, and financial resources.

- If you have an idea of which institutions are of interest to you, go to their websites and review their program offerings. Usually, typing www.*nameofinstitution*.edu in your web browser address bar, where *nameofinstitution* is the name of the institution in question, will direct you to the institution's website. You can also use a search engine to search for the institution.

- Visit the websites for various professional organizations for information about nursing programs—for example, Sigma (https://www.sigmanursing.org) and the American Nurses Association (https://www.nursingworld.org). It's also a good idea to explore these and other professional websites to find out where their leaders received *their* degrees. This can give you some ideas of programs that might meet your needs.

- Check out the websites of the numerous publications that list and rank colleges and universities. These include the websites for *U.S. News & World Report* (https://www.usnews.com) and *Peterson's Complete Guide to Colleges* (https://www.petersons.com).

- Explore state-run websites listing colleges and universities in your geographical area.

Tip

It is normal to vacillate during this phase. Don't be afraid to change your thinking; better to do it now than after you have begun your course of study. Part of this process is saying out loud what you want to do with your education and career so you can be sure you are taking the right path to that goal!

STEP 3: EXPLORING PROGRAM OFFERINGS

After you have identified the degree you want to pursue and any colleges or universities that offer that degree, you are ready to assess their program offerings. Each degree-granting program will have a slightly different emphasis and path, with different expectations and outcomes. As you move forward in this process, you should explore these differences to determine which program is best for you. Here are some points to consider about each program:

- What is the program's curriculum?

- Does the program's curriculum meet your needs?

- Is the program online or are you required to attend classes in person?

- Is there a residency requirement?

- Where is the college or university that offers the program?

- Will you have to move to attend classes? If so, have you factored in the cost and personal/professional expense of moving?

- Does the program allow for both full-time and part-time students?

- Are you required to complete the program in a prescribed time frame—for example, in four years?

- Does the faculty have a good reputation?

- Is the school you are considering attending particularly well-known in your area of study?

- What type of financial assistance (if any) is available through the institution or the government—for example, tuition reimbursement, stipends, nurse traineeships, scholarships, or student loans?

- Are you eligible for an educational loan from a bank?

> **Tip**
>
> Create a binder—for papers, online, or both—to keep track of any documents you acquire during the course of your research. That way, if you want to review something in more depth, share it with a colleague or mentor, or refer to it prior to an interview, you can find it easily.

Some institutions offer bridge programs—for example, from an associate degree in nursing (ASN) to a master's degree or from a BSN to a PhD or DNP. There are master's first-entry programs that are similar to graduate entry programs for individuals who have bachelor's degrees in non-nursing areas and who are pursuing their first nursing degree.

STEP 4: NARROWING DOWN YOUR OPTIONS

After you acquire all the necessary information about the degree you are interested in seeking and the institutions that offer that degree, it's time to narrow down your options. The goal here is to pinpoint the top five programs that meet your needs and interests, with one or two alternatives.

The best way to narrow down your options is to consider why you want to further your education in the first place and what factors play a part in that decision—namely, personal, professional, and financial factors. Closely examine each program of interest to determine which ones fit best when you take into consideration all aspects of your personal and professional life.

> **Tip**
>
> Going back to school can be a scary proposition for *any* professional. Take your time, do your homework, and ask for assistance from colleagues, peers, mentors, and experts whenever possible!

STEP 5: "INTERVIEWING" THE PROGRAM

After you have narrowed down your options, pinpointing the programs that you want to explore further, make arrangements to "interview" each one. This involves speaking to a faculty member or administrator on the phone, virtually, or, if you live nearby, in person.

Interviewing each program on your list gives you an opportunity to fill in any gaps in your knowledge before you make your final decision about where to apply. So, it's up to you to come prepared with questions. What do you want to know about the program, faculty, and resources at the institution?

It's particularly important to ask about any prerequisites for the program. Are there any classes you need to complete or standardized tests you need to take, like the Graduate Record Examination or something similar, before you apply for the program? Also inquire about the application process, including the dates for submission of all materials. Some schools have a rolling admission process, meaning they review applications as they are submitted; other schools have deadlines for applications to be submitted.

Note

If you are interviewing during COVID-19 (or a similar event), a program's normal communication procedures may be altered. Be flexible and expect to do a lot of the communication virtually—at least for now.

Tip

Interviewing the program will not only assist you in your decision-making process but also provide evidence to anyone at the school with whom you speak of your serious interest in the program.

STEP 6: COMPLETING THE APPLICATION PROCESS

You have collected all your information, reviewed it from every angle and with every factor and consideration in mind, and decided which program(s) you will apply for. Now you are ready to begin the application process. This involves filling out a series of forms provided by the institution in question.

> **Tip**
>
> Most colleges and universities require you to submit your application on-line, so be sure you factor that time in as you complete each application. Also be sure the institution wants you to fill out a specific application for its program versus a universal application that can then be sent to many programs for which you might be applying.

As you fill out your application for each institution for which you want to apply, keep these points in mind:

- Keep the directions for each application you want to fill out on hand and refer to them often. Anyone reviewing your application will consider your failure to follow these directions to be a big red flag.

- Know when each part of the application is due and meet your deadlines. If you can be a few days early, that is even better and means less stress on you.

- Spend adequate time on the essay component. Don't just crank it out and send it off. The essay reflects you as a person *and* a professional; be sure it shows you in the best possible light.

- Forward any necessary information about prerequisites—including (but not limited to) grades for prerequisite courses and scores for any required tests—to the college or university in a timely manner.

Some institutions require you to include letters of recommendation with your application. If that's the case, ask the people whom you want to write these letters well in advance to give them ample time to compose them. Also, provide these individuals with your resumé or CV for background information. If they need to submit their letter of recommendation online, provide them with the necessary login information or

> **Tip**
>
> If you have questions about the submission process, contact the school before you begin the application process.

give their email address to the admissions office if the form is to be sent directly to them.

STEP 7: CHOOSING YOUR PROGRAM

You have applied to the schools that best meet your needs, and several of them have accepted you into their program. Now it's time to decide what school you want to attend. To make your decision, ask yourself the following questions:

- Which program meets your needs the most completely?

- Which program has the most flexibility to accommodate your needs and interests?

- Which program will provide you with the best financial package?

- Which program has the best mentors in your area of interest?

- Which program will best prepare you to continue your career journey?

With the answers to these questions in hand, you will be prepared to make the best decision possible.

CLOSING THOUGHTS

Furthering your education through a formal program of study should not be taken lightly. Formal education is a commitment in time and money and often involves short-term personal and professional sacrifices. In the end, however, the education you receive will enable you to move forward on your career path and advance your career.

Determining what degree program you want to pursue and the best place to obtain that degree involves much thought, reflection, and research—including advice from people you respect in your personal and professional life. Whether you are completing a BSN degree, entering nursing as an accelerated-option student, pursuing an advanced practice degree, or working toward a terminal degree, you should make the best decision for *you*.

REFERENCES

American Association of Colleges of Nursing. (2001). *Indicators of quality in research-focused doctoral programs in nursing.* https://www.aacnnursing.org/Portals/42/News/Position-Statements/Doctoral-Indicators.pdf

American Association of Colleges of Nursing. (2006). *AACN statement of support for clinical nurse specialists.* https://www.aacnnursing.org/Portals/42/News/Position-Statements/CNS.pdf

American Association of Colleges of Nursing. (2015). *The doctor of nursing practice: Current issues and clarifying recommendations.* https://www.aacnnursing.org/Portals/42/DNP/DNP-Implementation.pdf

National Organization of Nurse Practitioner Faculties. (2018). *The doctor of nursing practice degree: Entry to nurse practitioner practice by 2025.* https://cdn.ymaws.com/www.nonpf.org/resource/resmgr/dnp/v3_05.2018_NONPF_DNP_Stateme.pdf

5

PROFESSIONAL DEVELOPMENT AND CONTINUING EDUCATION: ROLE EXPANSION

"Everyone I work with keeps adding letters to their signature, getting certifications in areas I never thought about. I am a bachelor's-prepared nurse with 10 years of experience in the neonatal intensive care unit. I have learned so much in my career so far and I apply it every day I work with my babies and families. Why do I need extra letters after my name to make a statement to others? I have asked my nursing colleagues and friends as to why they got certified in one area or another and their responses are never the same. Some tell me it was required by their unit or organization; others tell me that certifications helped them advance up their clinical ladder faster; still others said they got a 'small bump' in their hourly wages. I then asked a mentor of mine whose opinion I value, and he told me that obtaining certification should be about me and promoting my career first and foremost for myself. I thought about that for a week or so and decided to at least explore the certification exam for neonatal nurses. I weighed the pros and cons and, well, I did it, and I did it for me."

–R. A., BSN, CCRN-Neonatal

"I am lucky enough to be a delegate for my chapter of Sigma Theta Tau International. At the Biennium Convention in 2019, I attended the entire conference. I was so excited to interact with members from around the world, especially since I had never been to a conference like this before. I saw amazing poster presentations, stimulating podium presentations and panels, and so much more. I even got career advice in the Career Center. I was overwhelmed by all the information I took away from the conference and the profession and organization I belonged to as a fairly new nurse. I know that a lot of what I heard and saw I will be able to use in my career. So excited to keep learning in this way."

–K. H., BSN, RN

ADDITIONAL AVENUES OF CAREER ADVANCEMENT

Many nurses cannot or simply do not want to return to school for a formal program of study. Instead, these nurses might prefer to advance their career through other means. These could include the following:

- Continuing with educational coursework

- Taking certification exams and attaining advanced credentials

- Participating in professional or research conferences at the local, state, national, or international level

- Attending and participating in online programs/academies

- Participating in programs offered at their place of employment

- Volunteering as a preceptor or mentor

Tip

A certificate program is different from certification. When you complete a *certificate program,* you receive a certificate indicating successful completion of the program. *Certification,* on the other hand, entails passing a standardized examination given by a credentialing body and then being able to acknowledge your success by using the appropriate credential(s) after your signature.

ABCS OF EDUCATIONAL AND PROGRAMMATIC TERMS

A Accredited

B Board-certified

C Credentialed

D Development of skills

E Experts and expansion of knowledge/skill

F Fits career goals

WHERE SHOULD YOU BEGIN?

When you consider advancing your career through professional development courses, continuing education, or conferences, think about your ultimate goal. What do you want to achieve? To focus your thinking, ask yourself these questions:

- Do you want to expand your role?

- Do you want to expand your knowledge and skill set in a specific area?

- Do you want to advance as a clinician, educator, administrator, or something similar?

- Do you want to develop your skills as a nurse leader?

- Do you want to develop your research skills to integrate evidence-based research into your clinical practice?

- Do you want to become certified? If yes, in what area?

- Are you interested in receiving continuing education credits, a certificate of some type, or both?

- Do you want to enhance your credentials?

- What time frame are you considering?

- What time limitations, if any, do you have?

- Are you interested in a course that is more structured or unstructured?

- Are you an independent learner?

- What financial considerations, if any, do you have?

- Will you need additional resources to complete the coursework (e.g., a computer, books, or review materials)?

- Do you need to complete any prerequisite courses or obtain any prerequisite knowledge?

- Are you considering taking on this professional development project for yourself or to satisfy a recommendation or requirement issued by someone else?

Answering these questions will help you determine both what area you want to study and what type of coursework or conference is right for you.

FINDING COURSES, PROGRAMS, AND ACADEMIES

If you have decided that attending a course, program, or academy is the best way to further your career, your next step is to search for courses that will meet your needs. Explore all options in your area of interest, be it clinical, education, research, administration, leadership, or something else. The following sidebar contains some resources to help you get started.

 Tip

Think about whether you want to take a single course or to enroll in a program that might entail three or four courses. Also think about the time commitment involved—from a one-hour session to a program or academy that lasts for three to six months or something similar.

Tip

When searching for professional development or continuing education courses, use a variety of resources. Word of mouth, professional organizations, college and university websites, and internet searches are all great sources of information.

CAREER BYTE: RESOURCES FOR ADDITIONAL EDUCATION

Clinical: Oncology Nursing Programs/Courses

- https://www.ons.org/develop-your-career/professional-development?ref=HP

Clinical: Pediatric/Child Health Nursing Programs/Courses

- https://www.napnap.org/continuing-education/

Clinical: Critical Care Nursing

- https://www.aacn.org/education

Clinical: Advanced Practice Certificates

- https://www.aanp.org/student-resources/np-certification

Education

- https://www.sigmanursing.org/learn-grow/education
- https://www.sigmanursing.org/learn-grow/sigma-academies
- https://www.aacnnursing.org/
- http://www.nln.org/professional-development-programs
- https://www.nursing.pitt.edu/degree-programs/certificates/nursing-education-certificate
- https://www.nursing.pitt.edu/degree-programs/certificates/nursing-informatics-certificate-online

Research

- https://www.sigmanursing.org/advance-elevate/research
- https://fuld.nursing.osu.edu/ebp-certificate
- https://www.iacrn.org/
- https://acrpnet.org/certifications/

Administration

- https://www.aonl.org/education/overview
- https://www.nadona.org/
- https://www.sigmanursing.org/learn-grow/sigma-academies

Leadership

- https://www.sigmanursing.org/learn-grow/sigma-academies/new-academic-leadership-academy
- https://www.sigmanursing.org/learn-grow/sigma-academies/experienced-academic-leadership-academy
- https://www.sigmanursing.org/learn-grow/sigma-academies/nurse-leadership-academy-for-practice
- https://www.aonl.org/initiatives/cnml

ATTENDING CONFERENCES

Attending professional development or continuing education courses is one very productive way for nurses to advance their careers. Another way is to attend professional, research, or scientific conferences. Attending conferences—whether in person or virtually—is a great way to expand your horizons. Whether you are an attendee, a presenter, a panelist, or a volunteer, the experience of attending conferences can be career enhancing or even career changing.

When researching conferences to decide which one to attend, think outside the box. Whenever possible, look for conferences in all geographical areas—local, state, national, and international. Also, consider attending conferences outside your normal topic area.

Tip

In addition to helping nurses increase their knowledge in an area of interest, conferences enable them to network with other professionals, both inside and outside of nursing. These contacts can lead to other formal and informal educational opportunities.

If you're constrained geographically, consider attending an online webinar. Numerous professional organizations, clinical agencies, colleges and universities, and healthcare organizations conduct webinars. Some people might want to participate in a webinar but are intimidated by the technology. If that sounds like you, find someone who can help you get set up. Better yet, have a webinar party! Invite your colleagues—including some who are more technologically savvy than you. Not only will you absorb the content presented in the webinar, but you'll also learn how to use your computer to enhance your career.

Tip

Don't be intimidated by technology. Trying new things and expanding beyond your comfort zone are part of growing as a professional. And don't think that your ability to work with technology is based on your age. It is not. Some individuals are just more technologically proficient than others.

VIRTUAL CONFERENCES IN THE TIME OF COVID

In-person conferences were put on hold during the COVID-19 pandemic, but virtual conferences have taken place. While the virtual-conference experience is different from the in-person experience, learning and networking can still happen.

During the pandemic, most professional organizations have made every effort to offer virtual conferences for presenters and attendees. They provide links, offer technological assistance if you need it, and generally make recordings available within 48 hours of the conference.

If you are attending a conference virtually, don't be inhibited. Maintain a presence, ask questions of presenters, engage in discussions, attend special offerings (such as the Sigma Career Center and exhibit halls), volunteer, and most importantly, enjoy the experience!

You're not limited to participating in a conference as an attendee. You can also be a presenter. Presenting what you know to others is a great way to learn, grow, and network. Yes, it might seem terrifying or even impossible, but that doesn't mean it's beyond your capabilities. Often, the conference's organizing body has resources available online to help you develop your presentation. You can also get help from a colleague, peer, or mentor. Remember: If you never try to do something new or scary, you will never know if you can achieve your goals!

CERTIFICATION AND CREDENTIALING

One way to provide evidence of your knowledge and skill is to pass a certification examination in your area of expertise. After you successfully complete a certification examination, the appropriate credentials can be ascribed to your name.

Being certified and credentialed provides both an internal and external evaluation of your abilities. Indeed, in many professional situations, certification and credentialing are components of the evaluation process and can affect your annual monetary and non-monetary compensation.

Certification examinations are available in such diverse areas as basic and advanced clinical practice, nursing education, nursing management, nursing administration, and nursing leadership. Additionally, there are specific clinical areas in which you can become certified—for example, chemotherapy administration or advanced cardiac life support.

To find out what certification examinations are available to you, begin by searching sites such as the American Nurses Credentialing Center at https://www.nursingworld.org/our-certifications/ and the Institute for Credentialing Excellence at https://www.credentialingexcellence.org/.

If receiving credentials from your organizing body is important to you, you should consider taking that organization's certification examinations when available. If your organizing body does not administer certification examinations in your area of expertise, seek out the diverse certification examinations offered by more broad certifying agencies.

> **Tip**
> Be sure that the organization that administers the certification examination you are considering taking is reputable and well-respected. You want to be certain that your credentials will be recognized by the nursing profession!

In addition, attempt to locate resources from your professional organization. For example, if you are a pediatric nurse or pediatric nurse practitioner, you would want to check out the website for the National Association of Pediatric Nurse Practitioners at https://www.napnap.org.

If nursing education is your area of expertise, the National League for Nursing administers a certification examination that, when successfully completed, makes you a Certified Nurse Educator (http://www.nln.org/facultycertification/index.htm).

> **Tip**
> You can do an internet search to find other organizations that administer certification examinations.

No matter what your area of expertise, there are several important points to consider with respect to certification:

- Do your research and find the examination that is right for you. No one knows you or your expertise better than you do, so let that guide you in your search.

- Use any resources provided or recommended by the administering organization to study for the examination. Even the most proficient professional should review prior to the examination!

- If for some reason you are not successful in obtaining a certification, look at it as a bump in the road—a learning experience, not a failure. Even the most proficient professional can have an off day.

- Once you are successful, pay it forward. Teach a class for the next certification examination period for your colleagues or tutor others who are not the best at standardized test taking.

CONCLUSION

Of course, one way to advance your career is to seek a degree in a formal program of study from a college or university, as discussed in Chapter 4. But for various reasons—including personal and professional commitments, financial considerations, and more—not all nurses can or want to go that route. For them, professional development, continuing education courses, conferences, or certification examinations might be a better fit. Advancing your career through these means benefits you, your colleagues, your patients, and the nursing profession. Whatever path you choose, researching the various avenues to meet your goals and implementing your plan with purpose are key to your success.

6

THE VALUE OF MENTORSHIP: A TWO-WAY PROCESS TO PAY IT FORWARD

With Contributing Author Samantha Martin, BA

"The mentor-mentee relationship is an essential component for professional development. As a mentee, I was impressed by my mentor's passion for nursing and expertise in the field. My mentor was deeply committed to mentoring and supporting her mentees toward becoming future nurse innovators and leaders. She truly embodied the full scope of a nurse who is innovative and seeks to mentor others. Our mentoring sessions have had a significant impact on my career path and decisions. I personally believe she was a phenomenal mentor. Her efforts were driven by a desire to operationalize my personal mission and vision. Through this transformative process, she supported me in understanding their purpose and the value they bring to the profession. Throughout the mentoring process, I felt empowered to take ownership of my professional journey. My mentor consistently made herself accessible and available to work through and support various professional decisions. She has had a significant impact on my career as an educator and researcher. Her feedback was insightful and has helped shape my program of research and teaching philosophy. Despite her overwhelming and demanding work schedule, my mentor consistently found ways to support me with my nursing career, including during the COVID-19 pandemic. She consistently followed up to ensure that she had addressed questions and responded quickly to requests for additional information. Her willingness and commitment to mentorship, education, and supporting others is unequaled. I am thankful that I have the opportunity to work with such an icon in the nursing profession."

–L. L-P, Ed.D-CL, MSN, RN

*"In my 43 years as a professional nurse and educator,
I have mentored many students and colleagues in areas
such as finding their first practice opportunity, how to
assimilate to one's role, what steps to take next on their
career path, and how to be an effective educator, researcher, writer, and mentor. I mentor mid-career nurses in the
overall process of changing career trajectories, dissemination of their works through publications, presentations,
and writing grant applications. I mentor doctoral students
as they learn to navigate the world of academics, research,
and the 'new' opportunities they will be able to explore.
I mentor nurses at the end of their formal careers in areas
related to giving back to the profession outside of their
past environment, becoming entrepreneurs, and using their
'voice' as a means of change. I have been mentored in
many of these same areas along my career trajectory. My
mentors have included my mother, a registered nurse who
taught me how to apply theory to enhance my clinical
practice; a former faculty member, who taught me how to
educate students from diverse backgrounds; and a nurse
leader, who taught me how to navigate the broader world
of professional nursing. I have learned from many who
have mentored me how to use my 'voice' to disseminate
and to make change in the world of nursing and healthcare. I have been lucky that even after 43 years as a nurse,
I still have opportunities to learn from mentors who are
constantly teaching me, pushing me, challenging me, and
guiding me in being the best version of myself as a professional nurse. I have taken what I have learned from both
my mentor and mentee roles and used all of the lessons as
I continue to mentor today. As I pay it forward, I hope
that future mentors will arise from my contributions."*

–L. M., PhD, MN, RN

MENTORSHIP DEFINED

Nurses have had mentors since the time of Florence Nightingale. Indeed, mentorship has been around as long as there have been nurses. *Mentorship* constitutes a relationship between a more-experienced individual and a less-experienced individual. Mentorship is a two-way partnership in which the mentor effects the desired change outlined by the mentee and inspires the mentee to take on new and exciting opportunities and challenges, complete tasks, develop skills, or pursue projects that are unfamiliar to them. At the same time, imparting knowledge and expertise to a mentee enables the mentor to grow and advance in their own career.

> *Note*
>
> Professional nurses can be mentees, mentors, or both at varied points on their career journey.

A mentorship relationship can be formal or informal. A formal mentorship relationship is one where an organization has matched mentor and mentee. Informal mentorship occurs when a relationship has developed over time and the mentor and mentee select each other.

When considering mentorship, it is important to note the differences that may be present between younger nursing professionals and more experienced ones. Age is irrelevant in this context; it's sharing experience and expertise with others that matters. Younger professionals often see mentorship as a goal-oriented transaction. For example, they ask, "Would you look at my resumé?" or, "Can you give me some tips on how to succeed in an interview?" Often, these "transactions" are more applicable to a coaching situation than a mentorship partnership. More-experienced nursing professionals typically view mentorship as a relationship—a career-long partnership. It's important to find the balance between these two views of mentorship as the process of working together begins.

MENTORING VERSUS COACHING

Mentoring is not the same as coaching. *Coaching* is generally viewed as a short-term relationship—less than three months—during which the two parties work on a specific task. *Mentoring* is more of a long-term relationship. This relationship usually lasts at least six months but can be longer depending on the goals agreed upon between the mentor and mentee. Some mentoring relationships are career-long and change with the ebbs and flows of both parties' careers.

Mentorship is antithetical to a common misperception about more-seasoned nurses—that they "eat their young." While there will be ineffective working relationships in any profession or job, including nursing, there are far more positive mentoring relationships between nursing professionals in every corner of the world.

> **Note**
>
> Paying it forward, or giving back to others in the profession, can be powerful, exciting, and satisfying.

THE BASICS: ROLES, RESPONSIBILITIES, PROCESS

The path you have taken in your career may enable you to serve as a mentor to others. Even early-career nurses can be mentors. After all, nursing students need mentors when they are in clinical settings, and new graduates need mentors who have recently gone through the experience of being a new nurse.

For their part, more-experienced nurses have much to offer others in practice, academics, policymaking, and so many other diverse areas and activities in which nurses participate during their careers. And nurse experts, who are perhaps at the end of their work careers, may be able to give more time to mentorship, as it's often the case that these nurses create their own schedules and make their own choices regarding how they spend their time at work.

> *Note*
>
> Becoming a mentor entails a time commitment. But if you have the time, the expertise you can provide as a mentor to another nursing professional is invaluable.

If you are a mentor, do not think that you can't also be a mentee. It might well be the case that you are experienced in some areas of nursing but a novice in other areas; that describes many of us in our careers. Seeking out a mentor to guide you and help you achieve goals in new and challenging areas is an opportunity not to be missed. Depending on your situation, you might take on the role of mentor, mentee, or both—yes, even at the same time.

A mentee should be viewed as the driver of the mentorship. They can't be passive. They must be an active participant in the relationship. The mentee can't enter the mentorship relationship thinking that the mentor is just going to hand them everything they are looking for. If they do, the relationship will not stand a chance of being successful.

A successful mentoring relationship consists of several essential elements:

- There must be a clear set of goals and objectives.

- The relationship must be a true partnership.

- The mentor and mentee should draft a formal agreement or contract so that both parties understand their roles and responsibilities as well as each other's expectations.

- A mentor and a mentee must be a good fit.

THE ABCS OF EFFECTIVE MENTORING CHARACTERISTICS

There is not just one definition of a good mentor and/or a good mentee. To be effective, the mentor and mentee each must possess some of the following characteristics:

	Mentor	Mentee
A	Advisor	Advisee, ambitious
B	Belief in mentoring abilities and the mentoring process	Belief in oneself and the mentoring process
C	Communicative, confidential, committed, and caring	Committed, "can-do" attitude
D	Desire to mentor, teach, and facilitate	Desire to be mentored, determined
E	Expert, empowered, evaluator	Eager, energized, encouraged
F	Facilitator	Fervent

The relationship must be such that both participants can benefit, grow, and advance in their careers from the experience. If there is lack of commitment, communication, or understanding of expectations, the risk of an unsuccessful mentorship increases. The success of a mentoring partnership also depends on participating in and valuing the evaluation process of the goals and objectives, as well as the overall relationship.

> **Note**
> Think about what role mentorship has played and will continue to play in your career as a mentor, a mentee, or both.

"Mentoring has long been a crucial part of nursing. Mentoring is most often applied to assist undergraduate students in their clinical placements in my experience in

Australia, although its application is extending to new nursing graduate employees and early career nurse educators and researchers. Traditionally, mentoring has taken place in a face-to-face format due to practical reasons. As technologies advance and the purpose of mentoring expands, mentoring nowadays can be undertaken via telephone or internet-based methods such as Skype, Zoom, Facebook, and Twitter. The most often mentioned benefits of mentoring are to facilitate professional development and to facilitate familiarization and culturalization into a new setting or workplace. At the same time, mentoring is a form of a professional relationship where the outcomes, either positive or negative, are much dependent on time, effort, and the attitude of both the mentor and the mentee. Background and contextual factors can also substantially influence the success or otherwise of mentoring. As the impact of mentoring can be profound and long-lasting, mentoring indeed requires a skill set to develop and an organization to support these efforts. If you are planning to seek help from a mentor or offer mentoring to someone, it is essential to take into consideration these personal, contextual, and organizational factors, and not to be forgotten, to maintain patience as well as an open mind."

–V. N., PhD, MN, BN

WHAT DO YOU GAIN FROM MENTORSHIP?

A mentorship experience has the advantage of being developed by the mentee and mentor to meet the specific needs of the mentee's career as set forth during their initial meeting. It is that uniqueness of mentorship that makes it so desirable as a means of career development, growth, and advancement.

The potential gains that can occur from a mentorship experience can be as wide and diverse as the two individuals involved in the partnership. The mentee can gain an enhanced professional skill set, as they define the specifics of that depending on their career position. Expansion of one's network for all things career and more is a real benefit of mentorship. You never know who you can connect with, whether you are the mentee or the mentor.

Mentorship can provide a door to new and exciting career opportunities. During your mentorship experience, your mentor or mentee might learn of a position for which you could be a potential fit. Or maybe through a contact or even a conference you attend together, your mentor or mentee might introduce you to someone who has an opportunity that would advance your career—sometimes even in ways you never considered. These types of opportunities might become available for both the mentee and the mentor, so do not think this is one-sided. The key is to always be open to opportunities, especially when they come about from a mentorship experience, where trust has been built.

> **Note**
> Mentorship experiences can assist both parties, but especially the mentee, to develop, promote, and enhance their nursing identity (discussed in Chapter 3).

Lastly, mentorship experiences can provide a support system that may have been lacking in your position or on your career path. Often, having a mentor that takes on the role of sounding board can be more beneficial than you could ever have expected. As nursing professionals, we inhabit the roles of caretaking, caregiving, and support, but often we don't have or seek out our own support systems. A mentor—or a mentee, for that matter—can provide you with the support and resources you need to move forward in your career. This in turn can promote resilience, empowerment, and career satisfaction.

> **Tip**
> Manage your expectations from the beginning of the mentorship experience. Once either party feels that expectations can't be met, doubt about the relationship can set in and lead to an unsuccessful partnership or one that ends abruptly.

"It is not easy to ask for help, and sometimes it's even harder to listen to help. My mentor is someone that is my friend but who can also be the push I need to do something that I need to do. She has pushed me to grow my career and pushed me out of my comfort zone."

–S. M., BA

IS BEING A MENTOR RIGHT FOR ME?

How do you know if becoming a mentor is right for you? Ask yourself the following questions. If the answer to these questions is yes, then you should explore mentoring opportunities:

- Do I have a desire to work with others to assist them in advancing their career?

- Do I want to take on the added responsibility of sharing my expertise?

- Do I want to devote my time, energy, and effort into someone else's learning?

- Do I know which characteristics make an effective mentor?

- Do I want to give back to the nursing profession through mentorship?

Remember, being a mentor does not preclude you from learning from the experience! Mentors should gain knowledge and experience from the partnership, just as the mentee does. Yes, you should volunteer to mentor someone else because you want to share your expertise but also because you want to learn from the process, to grow as a mentor, and to increase your abilities for further mentorship and similar experiences.

FINDING A MENTOR

Finding a mentor can be more challenging than you might think. You want to find someone who has the characteristics mentioned in the preceding section, but you also want to find a person you feel comfortable with, who will challenge you, and who will support you in your efforts.

Finding a mentor begins with you doing some research into individuals who might be best suited to help you achieve your goals during the mentorship relationship. Because of advances in technology, your mentor does not have to be in the same geographical location as you, unless that is a characteristic of the relationship that is important to you. With all the advances in communication technology on a global scale, a mentee might find that the best mentor lives in the next state or region or even on the other side of the world—although in that case, time zones might become an issue, and that should be addressed at the beginning of the mentorship experience.

When your search for a mentor begins, have an idea in mind of how you would describe a mentor who would be a good fit for you and your goals. Think about the expectations you have for that person and what qualifications and characteristics you would like them to embody in relation to your needs. Choosing a mentor should not be taken lightly. This is a person who will influence and affect your career—hopefully in a positive way!

When searching for a mentor, there are several avenues to explore. For example:

- **Professional organizations:** See if any professional organizations you belong to have mentorship programs. For example, Sigma Theta Tau International offers several mentorship programs through the Mentorship Cohort and the Mentorship Mini-Academy. In addition, hundreds of Sigma members have volunteered to be mentors in the many diverse areas of professional nursing available on Sigma's Career Center. Other professional organizations may also offer mentorship programs. Often, these programs relate specifically to the focus of the organization. Be sure that the focus is one that matches what you are looking for in a mentor.

CHOOSING THE RIGHT MENTOR

Things to consider when choosing a mentor include the following:

- Area of interest

- Specialty area, if applicable

- Preferred method of communication

- Career stage

- Geographic location

- Language preference

- Time commitment

As a mentee, consider which of these are most important to you in a mentoring relationship, and choose your mentor accordingly. Be honest with yourself. Do not ignore your concerns when choosing a mentor. If you do, you might later discover that the relationship does not work—for example, because you can't find a time to connect, a language you are both comfortable speaking, and/or the communication method that works best for both of you (face-to-face, phone, or internet).

- **Professional and/or clinical conferences and meetings:** Maybe you will engage with someone whose presentation was of interest to you. Or you might meet someone who is doing research in the same area as you and lives nearby so you can connect in person (once the pandemic has ended). Or you could be introduced to a potential mentor from a colleague you are talking to during a virtual conference. But that's not all. You might also find a potential mentor by reviewing conference proceedings and/or publications.

- **Your professional colleagues and personal contacts:** These can be great sources for finding a mentor. Remember, each person you know has their own network of contacts, and your future mentor might well be in that "web."

Tip

If you read a conference abstract or a publication that is in an area that you think is impactful, try emailing the author. You might find a mentor that way!

- **Social media:** You might find someone on social media who would be a good match for a mentor. To increase the likelihood of this happening, follow contacts of people you are already following, as they will generally have similar interests or careers to yours. Post on someone's page and start a discussion or comment on a post to launch an introductory conversation. Try asking individuals whom you already know or are familiar with on social media, "Do you know someone who . . . ?" This is always a good way to make contacts outside your normal career circle. You never know when that initial ask might lead you to a mentor.

If you ask someone to be your mentor and they decline, don't take it personally. Chances are the person simply can't take on added responsibilities at this time. But all is not lost. It is possible they may be able to connect you with another person who can meet your needs.

BUILDING YOUR MENTORSHIP PLAN

To begin your mentorship work, you must take three important initial steps:

1. **Develop a mentoring agreement or contract:** You must have a mentoring agreement or contract that outlines what the mentee and mentor expect of each other (see Appendix G for an example). This agreement should be composed by the mentee and then sent to the mentor for review and modifications. Once both the mentee and mentor agree on the contents, both parties should sign and date the agreement. This document should be viewed as binding by both parties. If one party does not meet the expectations outlined in the contract, then the agreement can be viewed as null and void.

2. **Create SMART goals and an action plan:** The mentee should work with the mentor to define goals and objectives that are specific and measurable. You can frame your goals and how you plan to accomplish them using the acronym SMART. (See the sidebar below on this topic.)

3. **Establish a means of evaluation:** If you set SMART goals, evaluating whether you have achieved them will be simple and effective.

SMART GOALS

The acronym SMART has been used for decades to assist in writing goals and objectives. Each goal or objective should be:

*   **Specific:** Goals should be described using clear and concise wording that indicates exactly what is to be accomplished.

*   **Measurable:** Goals should be measurable using objective versus subjective metrics and with a clear understanding of how and when the goal or objective will be achieved.

*   **Achievable:** Ensure that the stated goal or objective is feasible.

*   **Realistic:** Ensure that the end results desired are within reach.

*   **Time-bound:** Use a timeline or set due dates for when the goal should be achieved. If interim objectives are indicated, then dates as to when those will be met should also be included.

NEXT STEPS FOR YOU . . .

- Develop professional goals and objectives
- Complete a self-assessment of your career needs, short- and long-term
- Develop an action plan
- Explore opportunities for mentorship
- Make a connection
- Evaluate
- Pay it forward

TECHNIQUES TO PROMOTE SUCCESSFUL MENTORSHIP

After the mutual agreement or contract has been signed and the goals, objectives, expectations, and desirable outcomes have been established, the real work of mentorship begins. Mentorship is not a perfect process, and there may be ebbs and flows, but it is incumbent on both the mentor and mentee to do all they can to make the partnership a success. Both mentor and mentee need to be willing to make time, be flexible, and be committed to the process of mentorship.

One of the most important strategies for success is to build a trusting and honest partnership. Both the mentor and the mentee need to listen and hear, not just talk. Both parties need to be active participants. Demonstrating a willingness to communicate is key to a successful working relationship. It's particularly important for the mentor to be honest and open when discussing the mentee's strengths and weaknesses. At the same time, the mentee must be secure enough to accept constructive criticism as part of the learning and mentoring process.

In the post-relationship evaluation, it is critical for both the mentee and the mentor to give and take constructive criticism—not only to learn from the experience but to be able to take it with them to future mentoring partnerships.

Tip

One way to keep the mentorship experience on target is to work on one goal at each meeting. This will help both the mentor and the mentee to stay focused, remain cognizant of time, and evaluate the process so that any issues can be raised and modified in the next meeting.

POTENTIAL ROADBLOCKS TO MENTORSHIP SUCCESS

While the goal for any mentorship relationship is for it to be successful and mutually satisfying for both parties, there are instances in which the relationship may not be what was expected or fails altogether. Common roadblocks to mentorship success include but are not limited to:

- **The mentee:** As a mentee, consider how you are behaving within the mentorship relationship. Are you getting your work done in a timely manner? Are you keeping your meetings with your mentor? Are you meeting the responsibilities set forth in the mentorship contract? Don't be your own worst enemy! You made a commitment to become a mentee, so follow through. If for whatever reason you think you can't meet the mentor's expectations, be honest and forthright. Don't block yourself from learning from a mentor, and don't ruin opportunities for future mentorship by becoming known as someone who does not follow through.

- **Poor fit:** There may be instances when the mentorship partnership just isn't a good fit. This can be due to either the mentee or the mentor. Maybe the timing is off. Maybe your personalities clash— for example, one of you is a pragmatist and the other is a dreamer. Maybe the mentor just can't provide what the mentee is looking for. It's OK to acknowledge that the partnership is a bad fit! It often clears the way for the mentor to suggest someone who might work better. Either way, you can part ways amicably.

- **Other parties:** Sometimes other people can influence your mentorship partnership—for example, personal and professional acquaintances of either the mentee or the mentor who think it is OK to "give their two cents" about how the mentorship partnership is progressing.

- **Time:** Time can be an issue for one or both members of the mentorship partnership. For example, other higher-priority activities and/or responsibilities or unexpected life events can take time away from the mentorship partnership. Time could also become an issue if the mentee and mentor live in different time zones or have different work schedules.

- **Situational circumstances:** There are various situations that could affect the mentorship partnership. For example, the mentee's or mentor's professional position could change, one of them could be relocated, or one of them might find that new work responsibilities make it impossible to carry on with the relationship. Changes in someone's personal situation can also have an impact. Any of these could cause the mentorship partnership to be placed on the back burner for a specified time or even end altogether.

- **Lack of support or resources:** For some individuals, a lack of support by colleagues or superiors or by people in their personal lives can result in a roadblock—for example, if they put demands on you that prevent you from fulfilling the expectations of the mentorship partnership. Similarly, if you mentorship partnership requires that you have access to library resources, internet resources, and so on, the lack thereof can also become a roadblock.

Roadblocks to mentorship success may exist, but that does not mean that a mentorship partnership is not for you. If you hit a roadblock, don't give up. Seek out another mentorship partnership. Each partnership and experience will be different! Learn from each experience—good and not so good.

BUILDING A MENTORSHIP NETWORK

One of the benefits of participating in a mentorship relationship is the opportunity to build a mentorship network. You begin this process by connecting with your mentor's network of experts in areas that are related to your own areas for growth and development. If your mentor is not terribly familiar with an area of interest to you, or if your mentor has a colleague who can provide additional expertise, such a connection can be made.

Every time a mentee connects with an individual who can provide expertise, they should add that person to their network of mentors. You can also add to your network via your contacts on social media (e.g., LinkedIn or Twitter), by way of individuals you have met through various professional organizations or conferences, and by contacting the authors of research or publications you have read.

> **Tip**
>
> Do not be afraid to reach out and make a connection. Many times, it will lead to a person who can and will mentor you!

GLOBAL MENTORSHIP

"Australia is a large continent and island with the Pacific Ocean on our east coast and the Indian Ocean on our less-populated west coast. From the east coast we are 18 hours flying time to Los Angeles; a big stretch of ocean separates us from many nations and continents. An invitation to join the Sigma Global Leadership Mentorship Program changed my perception of geographic distance and its impact on forming meaningful connections. I was a new inductee to Sigma Theta Tau International when I was paired with a mentor in this program. With little

previous exposure to Sigma and being an early career academic, I was barely finding my feet in my local pond, let alone the big seas of the international nursing world. That was all about to change, and so much for the better. From our first encounter, where we discussed goals and logistics for our newly formed partnership, my mentor modeled a leadership style that was authentic, positive, and engaged, and her passion for nursing was inspirational. I would look forward to our fortnightly meetings, ready for feedback on how I went about implementing leadership strategies we had discussed. Even my local colleagues benefited from my mentor's recommendations. They would often ask what strategies we had discussed and how they were working out. The impact of our mentoring relationship was immediate, positive, and constructive, and quickly developed into a friendship that continues today. We are now working on a research project. Whilst the formal time in the program has ended, the wisdom I gained from watching and listening to my mentor interacting with myself and others continues to positively shape my approach to leadership. A gift indeed!"

–N. T., PhD, Master Ed. Studies, BN, RN, GCAP, FHEA

If you are interested in pursuing a mentor or mentee in another country, here are some steps you can take:

- **Become a member of an international nursing organization:** Organizations like Sigma Theta Tau International (http://www. sigmanursing.org) enable you to network in person and online with nursing professionals from around the globe—some who want to be mentored and others who want to mentor nurses with less experience than themselves.

- **Attend conferences:** These can be virtual or in-person (pandemic permitting). This enables you to connect with other nursing professionals from all over the world who share similar interests, perform similar research, or have expertise that you'd like to gain.

- **Join a structured mentor program:** Organizations like Sigma offer mentor programs through which you can be paired with a mentor or mentee from another country.

- **Perform a more informal search:** You can search through Sigma's list of mentors and mentees to match yourself with a mentor or mentee who lives abroad. You might need to approach several people before you find a match, but with perseverance, you can be successful with this approach.

- **Discuss mentorship possibilities with your local Sigma chapter:** You might be able to co-sponsor a mentoring program with a sister chapter somewhere else in the world that you can all benefit from.

- **Ask international colleagues:** If you work with colleagues or know other nursing professionals from other regions around the world, see if they can help you find a mentor or mentee from their area.

- **Read international nursing and other healthcare journals:** This can help you connect with foreign authors to discuss the possibility of a mentorship partnership.

- **Use social media:** Individuals all over the world often use social media to put out a call for a mentor or mentee.

Tip

If you find a global mentor or mentee, you will likely live in different time zones and have different work schedules. Be sure that you will be able to meet, in whatever way you determine, at a time that works for both of you.

Note

Each mentorship relationship is unique, with distinct characteristics based on the mentee and mentor in the partnership.

GLOBAL MENTORSHIP INITIATIVE EXAMPLE: IT BEGAN WITH AN IDEA . . .

With mentorship opportunities come the ability to address the diverse issues and needs we have in nursing on a global basis. One such program was developed by members of Sigma from around the world. The Global Leadership Mentoring Community was developed to provide a platform to engage and mentor emerging global leaders in Sigma's seven global regions. Sigma members, identified as coordinators, facilitate the community, with a focus on leadership development for other members who are interested in global nursing and in organizational leadership roles within Sigma. Individuals were asked to consider personal interests in conjunction with the Sigma mission and goals over a two-year period. Overall, research analysis on the program has shown successful outcomes related to the mentee's development as global leaders, despite some challenges related to differences in cultural perspectives, language, and communication across the world (Rosser et al., 2020). The program will continue to evolve as the need for global leadership in nursing is only going to continue to expand.

SOME FINAL WORDS OF ADVICE

All nursing professionals, no matter where they are in their career journeys and no matter how much they have achieved, may need advice, feedback, resources, and assistance when new and exciting challenges and opportunities present themselves. So, embrace the mentorship experience when you have the opportunity. Become a mentor, become a mentee, or do both. Mentorship experiences can affect and influence your career in more ways than you can ever imagine.

Note

Mentorship enhances your career, but perfection is not the goal. Always keep striving!

RESOURCES FOR INFORMATION ON MENTORSHIP PARTNERSHIPS

- "The Effectiveness and Application of Mentorship Programmes for Recently Registered Nurses: A Systematic Review," by C. M. Chen and M. F. Lou (2013, *Journal of Nursing Management*)

- "Empowerment and Mentoring in Nursing Academia," by M. D. Singh, F. B. Pilkington, and L. Patrick (*International Journal of Nursing Education Scholarship*, 2014)

- "Evaluating a Nurse Mentor Preparation Programme," by O. Gray and D. Brown (*British Journal of Nursing*, 2016)

- "Factors That Facilitate Registered Nurses in Their First-Line Nurse Manager Role," by K. Cziraki, C. McKey, G. Peachey, P. Baxter, and B. Flaherty (*Journal of Nursing Management*, 2014)

- "The Global Leadership Mentoring Community: Building Capacity Across Seven Global Regions," by E. Rosser et al. (*International Nursing Review*, 2020)

- "A Literature Review of Mentorship Programs in Academic Nursing," by L. Nowell, J. M. Norris, K. Mrklas, and D. E. White (*Journal of Professional Nursing*, 2017)

- "Mentor Satisfaction Using a New Model of Clinical Education," by L. A. Myler, C. L. Buch, B. M. Hagerty, M. Ferrari, and S. L. Murphy (*Nursing Education Perspectives*, 2014)

- "Mentoring as the Key to Minority Success in Nursing Education," by N. Crooks (*ABNF Journal*, 2013)

- "Mentoring in Nursing Education: Perceived Characteristics of Mentors and the Consequences of Mentorship," by S. Huybrecht, W. Loeckx, Y. Quaeyhaegens, D. De Tobel, and W. Mistiaen (*Nurse Education Today*, 2011)

- *Mentoring Today's Nurses: A Global Perspective for Success*, by S. M. Baxley, K. S. Ibitayo, and M. L. Bond (Sigma Theta Tau International, 2014)

- "Mentorship in Nursing Academia: A Systematic Review Protocol," by L. Nowell, D. E. White, K. Mrklas, and J. M. Norris (*Systematic Reviews*, 2015)

- "Mixed Methods Systematic Review Exploring Mentorship Outcomes in Nursing Academia," by L. Nowell, J. M. Norris, K. Mrklas, and D. E. White (*Journal of Advanced Nursing*, 2017)

- "Novice Nurse Faculty: In Search of a Mentor," by P. R. Cangelosi (*Nursing Education Perspectives*, 2014)

7

CAREER DEVELOPMENT AND MANAGEMENT FOR INTERNATIONAL NURSES

"I have always wanted to practice somewhere other than the United States, where I grew up and was educated. I love to travel and was lucky enough during my undergraduate college years to go on two mission trips to Ghana and study abroad in London, England. During these vastly different experiences, I learned that nursing and healthcare are very much dictated by surroundings, availability of services, governmental policies and laws, but most importantly by people and their circumstances in life. The challenges presented to people across the world related to health and illness are areas that I want to address. The thought of practicing nursing as a global nurse is exciting to me. Now I just need to figure out how to make that happen."

–E. C., MSN, ARNP-BC

"The world is large, and I like working in all of it when there is an opportunity for me. I currently work in the Middle East, but I have worked in the United States, where I am a citizen. I grew up in the northeast and went to undergraduate and graduate school in the south. Many years ago, an opportunity presented itself to work as a high-level administrator in a clinical organization and I took it. It has been an invigorating and challenging experience, but I am happy with the choice I made. Now I am considering making a change, but I am not sure what I want to do next or where I want to do it. Do I want to come back to the United States? Do I want to change my career trajectory? Are there interim steps or challenges I can take on while I try to figure this all out? I am not getting any younger."

–M. E., PhD, MBA, RN

SOME BACKGROUND

The ability to work as a professional nurse, in all the many paths we can take in our careers throughout the world, is both exciting and challenging. Some nurses just want to spread their wings—for example, moving from the US to other countries around the world. Other nurses elsewhere in the world want to move *to* the US to practice and/or continue their education. Still others want to make an impact on global nursing and healthcare but not necessarily with a geographical move.

The most common questions from nurses who practice internationally or those who want to do so are related primarily to these areas. Whether these questions are posed to me or to others through social media, via email after connecting at conferences, through networking opportunities, or through Sigma Theta Tau International (Sigma) and its global reach via the Sigma Career Center and in-person and virtual events, nurses are seeking guidance on working and practicing internationally, however they define that concept for themselves.

CULTURAL IMPACT ON CAREER DEVELOPMENT AND MANAGEMENT

For most international nurses, many of their common experiences are dictated by norms, cultural expectations, and organizational expectations in the country in which they practice. In a similar manner, how the inhabitants of a particular region perceive nursing and healthcare is often based on cultural norms and governmental policies and procedures. This is true for nurses across the globe.

It is incumbent upon you to research the area where you want to take your career journey so you are aware of what you should expect. This is true whether you are moving to North America or from North America to somewhere else in the world. You can find a lot of this type of information on country and embassy websites. But the most relevant information is often found by networking. Speak to peers, colleagues, friends, and members of relevant professional organizations who know the geographical area where you want to work to tap into their real-world knowledge and recommendations.

> **Tip**
> Do your due diligence in researching the regional, national, and organizational requirements and expectations when seeking a position, whether in clinical practice, academics, administration, government, or research.

If you are seeking a position abroad, frame your resumé, CV, and/or portfolio based on the requirements and expectations of the region and organization where you want to move and work to provide evidence that you understand the geographical location in which you are taking your career. (Refer to Chapters 1 and 2 for more information on writing your resumé, CV, and portfolio.) Of course, although the terminology and areas of emphasis in your resumé, CV, or portfolio might change depending on where you want to move, the purpose of these documents is still to present yourself as someone who brings unique qualities to the position for which you are applying.

"I have lived in the Philippines for all of my life. I will be graduating from nursing school with my BSN this year. I would really like to move to the US or Canada and practice there as a nurse. In my future I would also like to continue my education in one of those same countries. I have heard from a lot of friends that it is hard to get work abroad and that the process for moving and transitioning my education to North America is lengthy. I have a general idea as to what I have to do, from peers that have moved to the US and Canada, but now it is my turn and I want to be sure I do it all correctly."

–K. H., BSN nursing student

STAYING PUT . . . BUT BECOMING MORE ATTUNED TO YOUR ENVIRONMENT

If you are developing, growing, and/or maintaining your career journey but don't want to move geographically, you, too, may have career questions that are specific to the area in which you live. Ask for guidance from your colleagues, your mentors, your employer and/or your organization's website, and fellow members of professional and clinical organizations. In some cultures, asking for advice—including whom you ask for guidance— may be dictated by cultural norms. Be sure to conduct your inquiry within these norms if you want to obtain answers to your questions.

RELOCATING TO NORTH AMERICA

The most common questions asked by nurses who were educated and/ or work in countries outside of North America relate to their desire to move and work as a professional nurse in some capacity within the US or Canada. The primary issues related to such an international move involve having one's credentials evaluated and obtaining licensure as a registered nurse. Without addressing these first steps, any attempts to relocate to North America to work will be for naught.

As you begin the process of moving to North America, the Commission on Graduates of Foreign Nursing Students (https://www.cgfns.org) will be the primary source for answers to all your credential and certification evaluation questions. The FAQ page on this website (https://www.cgfns.org/faq/) can guide you through the process of receiving a comprehensive assessment of your records, whether you want to obtain your education in North America or you are already a nurse in another country and want to be licensed in the US or Canada. The "U.S. Nursing Licensure for Internationally Educated Nurses" page on the National Council of State Boards of Nursing website (https://www.ncsbn.org/171.htm) is another good source of information.

If you are a member of Sigma or other international professional organizations, talk to members within North America—particularly members who have made the same transition as you are planning—for additional tips and strategies. Those of you wishing to continue your education in North America can also find resources in International Studies departments at academic institutions.

SEEKING A POST-DOCTORAL FELLOWSHIP OR OTHER EDUCATION IN NORTH AMERICA

Professional nurses often inquire as to how to further their education in the US or Canada—including but not limited to seeking a post-doctoral fellowship. For anyone seeking such a position, research and networking are the keys to your success.

Find out which academic and/or clinical institutions are doing research in similar areas to yours. Are faculty and practitioners publishing on such research? If so, try to connect with the primary author via email to determine whether there are post-doctoral fellowships available—and most importantly, inquire as to whether these positions are open to international students.

In addition, ask colleagues or others in your research area who might assist you and where their colleagues have had successes. You can also use professional journals and other writings to find contacts with whom you might connect about a fellowship. But don't

> **Tip**
> You never know where a tip on a fellowship will come from! Never underestimate the importance of getting your name and interests out in the public domain for others to see.

stop there. Ask to tap into *their* network of colleagues in research positions and see what you can find.

Social media platforms, especially those with a large international member base, can be invaluable in finding a fellowship you are interested in pursuing. Follow or link to others with similar research interests and then follow the groups and individuals that they follow. Developing your own network by connecting with others via social media can expand your reach across the globe.

Do not be afraid to ask for guidance and direction from others when seeking a post-doctoral fellowship. Networking may be the best strategy to find a position, particularly for international students. Who you know, and who *they* know, may play a significant role in your obtaining the position you are seeking.

RELOCATION ACROSS THE GLOBE

Relocating to another country or region of the world can lead to many opportunities and exciting challenges. But it also can lead to difficulties and dismay—especially if you have not done your research ahead of your move.

USEFUL GOVERNMENT AGENCIES

If you need to find out whether a hospital or other type of organization requires a green card, visa, or similar, there are agencies that can assist you. Some countries have separate registration authorities that you can (or may be required to) contact. Here are a few good places to start:

- Nursing and Midwifery Board of Australia (https://www.nursingmidwiferyboard.gov.au/Accreditation/)

- Nursing and Midwifery Board of Ireland (https://nurseabroad.in/apply-for-nmbi-registration/)

- Nursing and Midwifery Council of the United Kingdom (https://www.nmc.org.uk/registration/search-the-register)

- South African Nursing Council (https://www.sanc.co.za/wp-content/uploads/2020/06/SANC-Revised-guidelines-Foreign-Registration-2016-05-15.pdf)

- Nursing Council of New Zealand (https://www.nursingcouncil.org.nz/IQN?WebsiteKey=fa279da8-a3b1-4dad-94af-2a67fe08c81b)

- Nursing Council of Hong Kong (https://www.nchk.org.hk/en/the_nursing_council_of_hong_kong/registration_and_enrolment_requirements/index.html)

Be sure you know the specific requirements and expectations of foreigners working as professional nurses in the country of your anticipated move. Inquire within governmental agencies or embassies in that country for assistance. For your country of interest, you must have a strong grasp of basic information about visas, passports, and nursing licensure requirements (and how to obtain them); working as a foreigner; housing opportunities; and any specifics related to available positions and requirements. For example, do you need a sponsor to work in another country? If so, where does that sponsorship come from, and for how long?

To practice internationally, you must have at least an associate's degree in nursing or a bachelor's degree in nursing. You will also need experience—although how much experience will depend on the position you are applying for and in what country. In addition, you will need to provide proof of licensure on the NCLEX-RN. Finally, you will need to provide proof of the states you have worked in as well as your resumé showing evidence of your experience.

It is always helpful if you speak the language of the country you want to practice in, including slang and local dialects. Although people in many countries do speak some English, it is likely *not* their primary language. To practice nursing effectively and efficiently, and to function as a member of the healthcare team, you must be at least familiar with, and preferably fluent in, the local language—not just the language for daily living but medical language that is unique to your role. Learning the language also shows your respect for the culture and practices of your colleagues and patients and enables you to better integrate into society.

Note

Of course, many healthcare organizations provide translators, and you can certainly use them when needed, but your comfort level and independence as a licensed professional nurse will be enhanced if you can communicate with patients, families, and colleagues in their own language.

LEARNING THE LANGUAGE

One way to learn a language is to use language programs like Rosetta Stone—although these might not help you gain a grasp of medical language. For that, it's a good idea to ask someone at the organization where you will be employed if they can recommend any resources to learn the language of nursing and healthcare for their country. If you're still not comfortable with your command of the language when you arrive in your new country, take advantage of translation applications on cellphones and other devices until you can get up to speed.

If you want to pursue nursing opportunities in a country where there is no reciprocal licensure, there are other possibilities for employment. For example, in Japan, there is no comparable licensure for nurses not educated in Japan, so if you want to work as a nurse there, you will need to take that country's own licensure examination—in Japanese. If you lack the language skills to do so, you could consider nursing employment opportunities with the US government in Japan (or any number of other countries) as a civilian at a military base. To find out more about these types of positions, see USAJOBS (https://www.usajobs.gov/) or the Global Health Jobs and Opportunities page on the Centers for Disease Control and Prevention website (https://www.cdc.gov/globalhealth/employment). You might also find opportunities through the Commissioned Corps of the U.S. Public Health Service (https://www.usphs.gov/).

A good way to find jobs abroad is to network with other nurses from around the world. You can do this by joining an international nursing organization such as Sigma (https://www.sigmanursing.org/) or the International Council of Nurses (https://www.icn.ch/). As a nursing professional, you can also work with healthcare recruiters who specialize in placing nurses in positions abroad. These recruiters will often assist you not only with obtaining a nursing position abroad but also with housing, banking, and so on. Just be sure the recruiter is reputable. Do your due diligence to find out about them, including talking to others who may have used their services previously.

Do not let the excitement of moving to another part of the world to work cloud your judgment or keep you from asking all the relevant questions. Seek out others who have made similar moves and ask for their tips, strategies, and pro-con lists. Look for nurse leaders in country-specific professional organizations, academic

> **Tip**
>
> What you are seeking might not be available in the way you expect in the country where you want to make a move. So, be open-minded to all possibilities that might interest you, but also know that it is OK to change your mind once you have done your research and examined all the ramifications of making a move.

leaders, and/or leaders in clinical organizations for advice and guidance. You want your decision to lead to a positive and impactful experience— not one that you regret!

SOME FINAL RECOMMENDATIONS

When considering a career change that involves an international move, it is incumbent on you to determine if everything is right for you: geographical location, time, position, employer, and circumstances. (Yes, as nurses, we always find the five rights!) To that end, here are some recommendations to help you determine if an international career move is an option you should consider:

- **Study abroad:** If you are still an undergraduate nursing student anywhere in the world and you have an opportunity to participate in a study abroad program—particularly in an area that you think you might want to live and work in at some point—enroll in that program. Study abroad programs, which are conducted by colleges and universities, are a great way to learn about a country and its healthcare system. If your program does not have a particular focus on nursing or healthcare, ask your faculty if they can assist you in arranging an experience in a clinical organization. Being immersed, even for a short time, in another culture and place may provide insight into whether this is something you want to consider once you have entered your nursing career.

- **Pursue international options within your educational program:** If you are further into your educational pursuits, inquire at your college or university if your program of study has an international component. For example, if you are working toward a dual master's degree in public health and nursing, find out what opportunities there are for international travel to care for clients or teach students. Every opportunity that you can partake in will give you the chance to see what your future might look like.

- **Take mission trips:** Participate in mission trips that are nursing or healthcare related. These are often conducted by schools of nursing or religious organizations. A religious organization is often the overarching sponsor or partner with a school of nursing or faculty member. No matter what point you are at in your nursing career, participating in a mission trip may lead you to determine that your future might lie in this geographical area or in the broader area of helping others through such mission trips.

- **Attend international professional conferences and participate in nursing or healthcare-related side trips:** Such opportunities can open your eyes to the possibilities for your future and how you might be able to use your unique abilities and characteristics to make an impact in a particular circumstance or country. If no official side trips are available during an international conference, connect with members of that country's chapter to seek out opportunities that they might be able to arrange for you or for a group.

- **Volunteer with international humanitarian organizations:** Contact Doctors Without Borders (https://www.doctorswithoutborders.org/), Nurses Without Borders (https://nwbfoundation.org/), and other humanitarian organizations where you can volunteer. These service opportunities can not only provide you with the great feeling of helping others but also give you a window into global opportunities that might be of interest to you.

- **Network:** Tap into colleagues, peers, and mentors who live and/or work internationally to find an opportunity that is of similar interest to you. You can connect with people through your current employer, your personal or professional network, professional organizations, or social media, just to name a few. The more information you can gather from individuals who are where you want to be—in location or position—the more informed decision you can make.

One final tip: Be careful when inquiring about or making an international career move. Make sure you are asking questions and obtaining information from reputable representatives, organizations, and sites, particularly on the internet. Double- and even triple-check the information you receive. Make direct contact with embassies/governmental agencies, potential employers, and agencies that assist with licensure, certification, and similar tasks. Making an international career move can be one of the best and most fulfilling decisions you will ever make. Just be sure to dot all your i's and cross all your t's!

8

USING SOCIAL MEDIA TO DEVELOP, AUGMENT, AND PROPEL YOUR CAREER

Author: Sarah E. Gray, DNP, RN, CEN, FAEN

"The entire social media boom is beyond me. I am older than most of my colleagues, and they are always on their phones or other devices, and I really have extraordinarily little idea as to what they are doing. I know that social media is important, as my grandchildren tell me, but why should it be important to me, and how can it help me, if at all, in my career? I understand LinkedIn, but I am not looking for a new position, so why do I need a profile? I hear nurses are using all sorts of social media sites for things I use my voice for on a call or via email. Am I missing something?"

–A. J., BSN, RN

LEVERAGING SOCIAL MEDIA

Social media has a role to play in your professional development. It's true that in the past, leaders and professionals did not need this tool. However, given the rapid evolution and growing influence of social media, failing to leverage it for professional purposes could mean that you are missing out on an important opportunity.

Developing a social media presence can contribute to your personal and professional brand. In simple terms, your *brand* is what you are known for, what you mean to people, and what people can expect when they interact with you. Your brand encompasses your in-person and online presence. This presence should be thoughtful and purposeful as you strive to meet your personal and professional goals now and in the future.

> *Note*
>
> Everyone has a brand—even you. However, not everyone consciously manages their brand. Whether you choose to do so is up to you.

Social media also plays a role in bringing together the collective voice of nurses on a global scale. Nursing association leaders often use social media to inform and influence political advocacy and policy. Social media can also be employed to organize the enormous nursing workforce to influence significant issues in healthcare such as climate change, concerns over work environments, and legislation affecting practice or licensing requirements.

Using social media, nurses can connect, share, and collaborate on innovations and emerging evidence—not just with each other, but also with like-minded communities in the healthcare industry. Innovations and emerging evidence are often outdated or no longer of interest by the time they appear in a print publication or conference presentation. Social media allows for the rapid and widespread distribution of this information, at little to no cost.

Finally, psychosocial support, recognition, and validation through social media can assist many nurses who face challenging situations or burnout, and spread positivity and hope. With social media, nurses can find camaraderie. Social media can be an ideal platform to continue conversations after an in-person conference, find research or publication partners, or discover self-care tips.

This chapter discusses the risks and benefits of social media, steps to identify the foundation of your brand, and practical tips to leverage your social media presence for professional development.

> *Note*
>
> It is clear there is value in engagement in social media by nursing professionals. It is also evident getting lost in the sea of social media can have negative effects.

RISKS OF SOCIAL MEDIA

Social media has become an everyday part of our lives. It has brought a level of transparency to our daily routines, beliefs, and interests we might not otherwise have with extended friends, friends of friends, and the public. However, social media comes with associated risks, as it can make us vulnerable to negativity and judgment or even compromise our safety and security. This section is meant to inform you of some (though not all) negative aspects of social media.

As a healthcare professional, you face risks associated with posting medical advice, violating patient or employee confidentiality, and engaging in unprofessional conduct. Your licensing body, employer, or volunteer affiliations may have policies in place to formally address these types of situations. Depending on the circumstances, you might also face legal action. Make sure you are aware of laws, policies, and practices that may affect your employment and affiliations.

> *Note*
>
> Your organization and even your profession have brands, and as an employee of that organization and a member of that profession, you are an extension of these brands. So, you must behave accordingly on social media.

In recent years, we have seen a significant amount of false information posted on social media, including information related to healthcare.

In February 2020, the World Health Organization cautioned that the COVID-19 pandemic had incited an immense "infodemic"—a plethora of information both accurate and inaccurate—making it challenging for people to identify reliable information (Pulido et al., 2020). Kumar and Shah (2018) suggest that educating people about possible manipulation tactics could "vaccinate" them against false information. In any case, it is imperative that healthcare professionals identify reliable resources and perform their own fact-checking to avoid contributing to the spread of false health information for the sake of public health and to build a reputable personal brand. A good rule of thumb is, if you can't verify something, don't share it.

THE EFFECT OF THE "INFODEMIC" ON MENTAL HEALTH

As mentioned, in 2020, the COVID-19 pandemic raised new concerns over the corresponding "infodemic" that occurred. So much information was being circulated that it was difficult for the public to discern factual information and recommendations from falsehoods. This raised concerns about the toll the excessive time spent searching for information played on mental health (Ni et al., 2020; Wong et al., 2021). However, it can also be concluded that by staying informed of the various falsehoods in circulation, caregivers could identify concerns shared among the public to mobilize more mental health resources (Ni et al., 2020).

There is evidence to suggest that social media can have a negative effect on mental health, although this evidence is mixed. Some research has shown that social media is a contributing factor to depression and anxiety (Ni et al., 2020), but other research has demonstrated the use of social media as a platform to *treat* mental health (Mehmet et al., 2020). It is true, however, that social media provides a veil of security *and* a public audience to those wishing to spread false, negative, and/or harmful comments.

Tip

Mentally and emotionally draining content, interactions, and news can have adverse effects whether consumed in person or on social media. Either way, to protect your well-being, do not waste time consuming content that does not add value for you.

BENEFITS OF SOCIAL MEDIA

Despite these risks, social media remains a valuable tool for professionals like you to convey your brand, bring together the collective voice of nurses, and build communities and networks for support and for the dissemination of evidence and research.

Social media offers a platform for you to convey or solidify your brand. Your brand is conveyed by things such as which social platform(s) you engage on, the groups and communities you engage with, and the content you post, like (or don't like), and share.

> **Note**
> Inattention and avoidance do not prevent your brand from existing!

The collective voice of the nursing profession is easily and quickly mobilized via social media. Nursing associations frequently use social media to inform members of the profession about legislation, laws, or standards that could affect practice. Informing nurses equips them to become advocates for themselves and for those they serve at the local, state, national, and global level.

Social media provides a way for you to expand your network. Your network is a valuable tool in your professional development and in the development of others. It is mutually beneficial to be connected. For example, suppose you have been tasked with planning an educational event, but you aren't sure where to find speakers or how best to engage your learners. Quickly searching your network or asking your network for recommendations may give you some useful ideas.

> **Note**
> Your network is a long-term investment. Over time, your connections might inform you of and even recommend you for new opportunities in employment, authorship, and presentations. Likewise, you might identify new opportunities for others.

Having a presence and engaging with others on social media can help you inform your network about your pursuits. This might prompt members of your network to recommend you for opportunities such as educational courses, articles, grants or scholarship funding, or events.

Building a network can also provide you and others with support and camaraderie. At some point in your professional journey, you might find your emotional and physical bucket near empty. Perhaps you will question your career choice or your ability to balance personal obligations with your profession. The bottom line is that you are not alone in these types of thoughts or feelings. By connecting with constructive groups on social media, nurses can offer or receive a kind word, give encouragement, celebrate victories, and share tips, resources, or personal anecdotes. This camaraderie is especially critical for new nurses as they move into the professional nursing practice environment and face challenges with family and friends who lack understanding of nursing work (Oneal et al., 2019).

Social media groups can aid in accountability, too. For example, many groups issue challenges on social media, which you might decide to take on. One group devoted to yoga for nurses recently issued a challenge to post when you had completed 10 minutes of mindfulness each day for a month. Each post was worth a point. Every person who attained a certain number of points by the end of the month was eligible to receive a free educational offering.

Speaking of accountability, I posted my mission and vision statements on my LinkedIn account profile. In doing so, I am holding myself accountable to those statements. In addition to representing my brand, these statements remind me of where I want to go and who I want to be each time I engage on social media.

Another benefit to social media is its ability to quickly disseminate research and evidence to a wide audience, including caregivers and the general public. Disseminating information on social media has its risks—specifically, spreading falsehoods. But nurses who know how to identify reliable sources and check facts beyond social media can both dispel false information *and* expedite the implementation of innovative techniques. In this way nurses can contribute to the health education of the public—especially in rural areas, where resources might be limited (Mehmet et al., 2020). On a related note, social media can also be an effective way to connect and share information among people with a similar diagnosis (Ryan & Sfar-Gandoura, 2018).

Sharing resources, articles, and timely evidence can be advantageous for nurses—especially when it relates to their own or related research. This can help strengthen their brand and increase their overall impact. Research and evidence are not conducted to sit on a shelf but to be implemented and improve the healthcare landscape. Moreover, scholarly debate on such posts can lead to further inquiry of thought and perhaps spark new research collaborations.

IDENTIFYING YOUR BRAND

A *brand* is a promise—an expectation of an experience. Brands are often associated with commercial entities, groups, or public figures, such as Apple, a political party, or Oprah Winfrey. Even if you are not selling a product or service, you still have a personal brand. Your personal brand communicates your unique identity and value. It is conveyed through in-person and online interactions, how you spend your time, your associated networks, and what you support or promote. This is true even if you are not actively managing your personal brand.

Designing and managing a brand—in person and on social media—can seem daunting. It's hard to know where to begin. As a first step, you must figure out who you are or who you want to be. You must also identify what your goals are for engaging in social media. Being deliberate will assist you in removing barriers to your success and help you manage your time. Taking this first step and crafting your brand is what this section is about.

Note

Be an authentic version of yourself, not a manufactured version to please others. Your brand should not be a second job; it is who you are—the authentic you.

WHO ARE YOU?

This simple question is enough to cause almost anyone to pause for reflection. Ultimately, though, answering this question really just means finishing these sentences:

- I am. . . .

- I value. . . .

- I dream about. . . .

- I spend my time. . . .

The best place to start with this is to identify your core values. *Core values* are guiding principles or fundamental beliefs that guide your behaviors and decisions. You can choose one or more methods to flush out your core values, depending on your personal style. For example:

- **Mind-mapping:** If you are a visual learner, this method is for you. Essentially, this involves brainstorming to create a visual map of you. This map could contain pictures, clippings from magazines, and all sorts of colors or arrows. You can add as much detail as you want. (See Figure 8.1.)

- **Making lists:** If you're more of a linguist, you might prefer to make a list to identify your core values. One way to do this is to search the internet for *core values list* or *character traits* to help you identify words that resonate with you. Identify 10 to 15 words or phrases that make you buzz; then narrow that list down to three to five words. Table 8.1 contains several words you might include in your list.

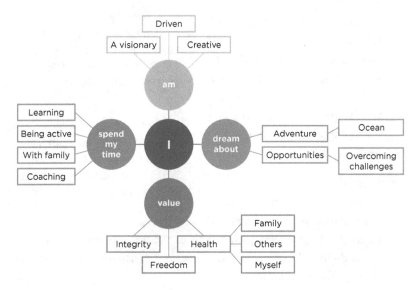

FIGURE 8.1 Visual mind-mapping.

TABLE 8.1 EXAMPLES OF CORE VALUES/CHARACTER TRAITS

Authenticity	Expression	Peace
Autonomy	Faith	Service
Balance	Family	Simplicity
Candor	Generosity	Success
Communication	Humility	Teamwork
Compassion	Innovation	Tenacity
Dependability	Justice	Trust
Dignity	Loyalty	Vitality
Empathy	Originality	Wealth

- **Completing surveys and taking quizzes:** Another way to help you pinpoint words or traits that embody you is by completing surveys and taking quizzes. You can choose from many options, but I like the Character Strength Survey by the VIA Institute on Character (https://www.viacharacter.org/ Character-Strengths-Survey). Use this survey as a tool to identify words that really speak to you. But don't stop there! Take the time to put it all together by journaling, as discussed in the next bullet.

> **Tip**
>
> When identifying your core values, don't overthink things. Let the process of pouring out your thoughts work!

> **Note**
>
> It is possible for your core values to change over time with major life experiences, but this is infrequent.

- **Journaling:** Use journaling to allow yourself to think freely. Then reread your thoughts and highlight themes. Next, use words or short phrases to identify those themes. Finally, review, refine, and consolidate your list into three to five core values.

WHO DO YOU SERVE OR WANT TO SERVE?

This question can be broad or narrow, depending on your preference. Either way, it might give you pause. For example, when thinking about who you currently serve, you might realize that it's not who you *want* to serve.

To figure out who you're currently serving, ask yourself these questions:

- Who are the greatest influencers of your vision?

- Who are the greatest influencers of your schedule?

Maybe the answers to these questions are a few groups or specific individuals. Maybe you're serving your employer, a specific patient population, or your fellow nurses. More broadly, you could be serving the global nursing community or healthcare providers.

In defining who you want to serve, you might consider other factors. For example:

- Faith

- Self

- Family

- Wealth

Again, this is something you can continue to refine.

WHERE ARE YOU GOING?

Put another way, who do you want to become or what do you want to accomplish? You can answer this by composing a vision statement. A *vision statement* describes your desired destination. As Timothy Gallwey writes in *The Inner Game of Work* (1999), "If you have a clear vision of where you want to go, you are not as easily distracted by the many possibilities and agendas that otherwise divert you" (p. 129).

"Begin with the end in mind," as Stephen Covey writes in his book, *The 7 Habits of Highly Effective People* (2013, p. 97). To that end, imagine what the world would look like if you achieved your vision. Ask yourself:

- What impact do you want to have on the population you serve?

- What do you want to be known for?

Your vision statement might be one sentence or a whole page. Either way, it should inspire you. If you aren't excited about where you are going, then what is the point of getting there?

> **Tip**
> When initially composing your vision statement, remember: You are not looking for perfection. You just want a working draft.

EXAMPLES OF VISION STATEMENTS

- "To be a published nurse who solves challenging problems in the field of technology." –Anonymous

- "To educate the public about how to optimize their health." –Anonymous

- "To have fun in my journey through life and learn from my mistakes." –Richard Branson, founder, Virgin Group

- "Not merely to survive, but to thrive; and to do so with some passion, some compassion, some humor, and some style." –Maya Angelou, poet

- "To help people find hope after loss." –Gloria Horsley, founder of Open to Hope

DESIGNING YOUR MISSION STATEMENT

A *mission statement* is written in present tense. It's a purposeful promise that focuses on how you will achieve your vision. When composing your mission statement, try to answer these questions:

- What do you need to do to achieve your vision?

- What can or do you provide to the population you serve?

- How will you make their lives better?

- Why do you exist?

- What is your purpose for today?

- At the end of the day, what do you hope you have achieved?

Tip

Evaluate and review your vision and mission statements at least every three months—if not daily—and revise them as needed. Ask yourself, are you making strides toward your vision? Are you adding value for those you serve?

EXAMPLES OF MISSION STATEMENTS:

- "My purpose is to equip and empower healthcare providers with the resources and opportunities they need to enhance their overall health and the health of all global communities."

- "My purpose is to use my creative talents to teach early-career nurses about the ways technology can propel their career and improve healthcare efficiency."

- "My purpose is to inform people on climate and global health issues and provide practical solutions."

- "My purpose is to provide an example of achieving balance between having a fulfilling career and being present for my family."

- "My purpose is to bring comfort and attentive care to patients at the end of their lives."

EVALUATING CURRENT AND FUTURE ENDEAVORS

By identifying and articulating your core values, vision statement, and mission statement, you create a lens to help you focus your energies. Focusing gives perspective to your professional and personal life so you don't feel like you are aimlessly wandering through life or spinning your wheels. Where are you spending your time? What committees, groups, or activities are you participating in that aren't serving your mission and vision? Are the activities you participate in supporting your purpose? Are you living someone else's vision by doing their to-do list?

You may have heard the phrase "Learn to say no." More specifically, learn to say no to endeavors that don't align with your goals, and maintain the capacity to say yes to the ones that do. If you consistently look through your own lens shaped by your core values, vision statement, and mission statement, it will be easier to identify what projects and initiatives will be fulfilling.

CHOOSING THE APPROPRIATE PLATFORMS

Social media is complex. When identifying ways to use social media to achieve your goals, you must be informed about the platforms you use. Begin by identifying one or two platforms to focus on. If you over-extend yourself, you probably won't be able to manage your social media presence well.

For many professionals, LinkedIn is the preferred social media platform. LinkedIn is a social network specifically for professionals to connect and showcase their skills, education, and professional interests. As of July 2021, LinkedIn hosts more than 774 million professionals in over 200 countries (Market.us, n.d.). Other social media sites that can assist you in advancing your career include (but are not limited to) Twitter and Facebook.

> **Tip**
>
> The key is to find the social media site or sites that work best for you in terms of what you want to contribute to them and what you want to get back.

PRACTICAL TIPS TO LEVERAGE YOUR SOCIAL MEDIA PRESENCE FOR PROFESSIONAL DEVELOPMENT

Regardless of what platform you choose to engage with, consider these tips to leverage your social media presence for professional development:

- **Use a respectable headshot for your profile picture:** It enables people to find you and makes you seem more trustworthy. Although it is nice to have a professional headshot done—on LinkedIn, users with professional headshots receive 21 times more profile views than those without (LinkedIn Help, n.d.)—a flattering selfie in professional clothing will also work well. Avoid using a group picture, a cartoon image, or a photo of a building.

- **Add a bio:** This enables others to recognize opportunities for interactions or collaborations with you. Your bio should add context to what you share in your profile. Add qualitative information when applicable. For example, instead of simply stating that you are "results-oriented," it is more effective to include actual numbers, such as grant dollars received, patient satisfaction scores you achieved, or the number of articles you have reviewed.

- **Engage with groups or experts with shared professional interests:** Follow and actively participate in professional groups on social media sites. Offering your expertise will help you build a reputation and help you gain insight into what others may be struggling with.

- **Do not be a robot:** Don't just like other people's posts (a practice known as *crowd surfing*). Add insight and value to them in addition to creating posts of your own. If you're not used to doing this, set a goal to add value or insight at least one or two times a week. This might mean posting a thought-provoking comment on an article or sharing an opportunity for continuing education with your followers and explaining why they might find it interesting.

- **Manage your contacts:** Social media platforms often recommend additional contacts who might interest you. Use this to your advantage. When you connect with someone, send them a personal message, such as, "Thank you for connecting. I saw you have a presentation coming up and I am looking forward to it." Adding a personal touch will help you develop your brand in the online environment the same way you would in person at an event such as a conference.

- **Connect your colleagues with others:** They might reciprocate the gesture, but even if they do not, you will feel fulfilled in having helped others.

- **Expand your network beyond your profession:** You need to network outside of nursing circles to make some of your most valued connections. Share your expertise with other groups—for example, physicians or marketing experts with similar interests. Just as you appreciate hearing the expertise of pharmacists or military personnel at your state or national nursing conferences, others will appreciate hearing your expertise. In fact, this can be a niche that sets your brand apart. In other words, by making these interprofessional contacts, you could become their go-to person for nursing- or healthcare-related opportunities, like political policy advocacy or board membership.

- **Do not get lost in the sea of information:** It is quite easy to be consumed and distracted by all the information posted on social media sites. Spend one to five minutes a week managing your social media contacts and posts. If you have additional time—for example, you are waiting for an appointment—you can look at posting more. You are not trying to create an online enterprise about yourself (unless that is your vision); you are simply attempting to create a framework that helps to promote your brand.

- **Put your posts through your brand filter:** You don't want your social media posts to hinder your success. Before you publish anything, ask yourself, does this post strengthen my brand? If not, don't publish it—especially if it could hurt your career. Along these same lines, stop any conversation that is going down the wrong track. The bottom line: Be professional and encouraging in every interaction.

- **Don't post angry:** Just as you should wait 24 hours before sending an angry email, you should hesitate before posting anything negative on social media. On a related note, while having professional debate is encouraged, be mindful if you are consistently using phrases like "In my opinion" or "Well, this is what I think." This is called applying an ego filter. Similarly, don't apply a fault filter—for example, placing blame or finding fault with everyone else's actions, posts, or dialogue.

- **Take stock:** Regularly assess your contributions, posts, and network on social media. Are you building your brand within your network? If not, adjust accordingly to ensure social media is a tool for your professional development.

ABCS OF MAKING AN IMPACT ON SOCIAL MEDIA

A   Authentic and articulate

B   Balanced

C   Concise, coherent, and contextual

D   Declarative

E   Expressive and explicable

F   Framed around central idea

CONCLUSION

Social media can connect the vast network of nurses and other professionals across the globe. Although there are risks and security considerations that you must understand before engaging in social media, it represents an opportunity for nurses to contribute to their personal and professional brand, meet their personal goals, add to the dialogue around professional nursing, share innovations and evidence, and provide support for one another. Identifying your core values and composing vision and mission statements provide a foundation for your brand, which allows for purposeful engagement rather than aimless clicking and scrolling. While opting out of using social media might not be detrimental to your professional development, leveraging this powerful tool could provide a wealth of opportunities.

REFERENCES

Covey, S. (2013). *The 7 habits of highly effective people: Powerful lessons in personal change*. Simon & Schuster.

Gallwey, T. W. (1999). *The inner game of work*. Random House.

Kumar, S., & Shah, N. (2018). *False information on web and social media: A survey*. Cornell University. https://arxiv.org/abs/1804.08559v1

LinkedIn Help. (n.d.). *LinkedIn public profile visibility*. https://www.linkedin.com/help/linkedin/answer/83?trk=hc-hp-shortcuts

Market.us. (n.d.). *LinkedIn statistics and facts*. https://market.us/statistics/social-media/linkedin/

Mehmet, M., Roberts, R., & Nayeem, T. (2020). Using digital and social media for health promotion: A social marketing approach for addressing co-morbid physical and mental health. *The Australian Journal of Rural Health, 28*(2), 149–158. https://doi.org/10.1111/ajr.12589

Ni, M. Y., Yang, L., Leung, C. M. C., Li, N., Yao, X. I., Wang, Y., Leung, G. M., Cowling, B. J., & Liao, Q. (2020). Mental health, risk factors, and social media use during the COVID-19 epidemic and cordon sanitaire among the community and health professionals in Wuhan, China: Cross-sectional survey. *Journal of Medical Internet Research Mental Health, 7*(5), e19009. https://doi.org/10.2196/19009

Oneal, G., Graves, J. M., Diede, T., Postma, J., Barbosa-Leiker, C., & Butterfield, P. (2019). Balance, health, and workplace safety: Experiences of new nurses in the context of total worker health. *Workplace Health & Safety, 67*(10), 520–528. https://doi.org/10.1177/2165079919833701

Pulido, C. M., Ruiz-Eugenio, L., Redondo-Sama, G., & Villarejo-Carballido, B. A. (2020). A new application of social impact in social media for overcoming fake news in health. *International Journal of Environmental Research and Public Health, 17*(7), 2430. https://doi.org/10.3390/ijerph17072430

Ryan, G., & Sfar-Gandoura, H. (2018). Disseminating research information through Facebook and Twitter (DRIFT): Presenting an evidence-based framework. *Nurse Researcher, 26*(1). https://doi.org/10.7748/nr.2018.e1562

Wong, F. H. C., Liu, T., Leung, D. K. Y., Zhang, A. Y., Au, W. S. H., Kwok, W. W., Shum, A. K. Y., Wong, G. H. Y., & Lum, T. Y. S. (2021). Consuming information related to COVID-19 on social media among older adults and its association with anxiety, social trust in information, and COVID-safe behaviors: Cross-sectional telephone survey. *Journal of Medical Internet Research, 23*(2), e26750. https://doi.org/10.2196/26570

9

EXPANDING YOUR REACH: USING YOUR VOICE

"I come from a very quiet family and background where speaking up, even in public, was not something I was comfortable with. Two years ago, at a professional conference, I went to a session on dissemination. I had been accepted to have my poster presented at the conference and I was excited and relieved that I would not have to speak in front of a large group of people. Someone who came to view my poster asked me a lot of questions and at the end of our conversation commented on how well I presented my study and findings. I realized from this experience and what I had heard in the dissemination session that no matter how you get your information to others, it is the fact that your work is contributing to others."

–K. C., DNP, RN

"As the issue of healthcare continues to grow in the public domain, I became an active listener of the discussions taking place at my state level, as well as the federal level. With the global impact of the COVID-19 pandemic this past year, and the lack of equitable delivery of healthcare services across the globe, my interest in politics and policymaking, nationally and internationally, has grown. I have become frustrated with the continued posturing of politicians and the use of healthcare reform as a talking point rather than an actionable and necessary change to be enacted. I have written to legislators in my state and in the US Congress, asking them to consider a nurse's perspective on all these critical issues. And yes, I hear back that nursing organizations are represented, but who and where are they involved and how much is their expertise valued? I see more nurses running for political office, but still, when do we hear them as invited guests on Sunday news shows or asked to write for news organizations? Where is the nursing expert who has a regular presence in the media as a healthcare contributor? These are the things I think about. This is where I want to make a difference currently in my career. I know that there are leaders who are working toward increasing the presence of nursing in the media and have read the Woodhull Report. I am educating myself as much as I can so that I can begin to let my voice be heard and listened to as my career takes on new meaning to me."

–F. W., PhD(c), BSN, RN

THE IMPORTANCE OF USING YOUR VOICE

Nurses often believe that they have nothing to offer to the discussions that occur on a daily basis in our professional lives or within the public discourse. But each of us possesses a unique perspective that is integrated into all the work we do in our specific area of nursing at different points on our career paths.

Sharing this perspective by using our voices—individually and collectively—is more important in today's healthcare and political environment than it has ever been. As the world continues to grapple with a pandemic and nations focus on healthcare issues that are specific to their citizens, it has become more and more evident that nurses' voices are needed in the public arena.

There are numerous ways to use your voice:

- Through dissemination of your work and expertise

- By being an advocate for the diverse groups of individuals with whom you interact professionally

- By becoming an active participant in professional organizations

- By becoming aware of and involved in the politics of the part of the world where you live and practice

Note

Your voice can potentially have an extensive reach. It is up to you how to take on the challenge of using your voice.

USING YOUR VOICE: DISSEMINATION

Your unique voice as a nursing professional is often first evident by the dissemination of your work. In its broadest sense, *dissemination* is the act of spreading information to a wider audience. In the context of nursing and the sciences, dissemination involves the presentation of data, process, and research/project findings to an interested and invested audience.

You can disseminate your expertise and work by:

- Delivering an oral or poster presentation or serving on a panel at a local, state, national, or international conference

- Writing an abstract

- Publishing a paper in a reputable print or online journal or other publication, including publications for nursing and healthcare professionals and for the public

- Engaging on social media, within mainstream media, and on webinars

- Serving as a consultant member of an organizational board or as an expert witness

As you can see, there are many ways for nursing professionals to extend the reach of their expertise and their work. It's up to you to decide how you will do that. For some of you, dissemination will be best done by using your written voice. For others, dissemination will be best done by using your verbal voice. It doesn't really matter *how* you disseminate— just that you *do*.

Dissemination is not always an easy process. For every success, there may be several failures—an abstract that was not accepted or webinar that was not well attended. But failure is a learning experience, and we all experience it at some points along our career journey. Give yourself permission to fail sometimes and take each failure as an opportunity to reflect and learn. Then go out there and try again.

> **Note**
>
> No matter what stage you are in your nursing career, from new graduate to retirement, you should share your voice as it relates to your professional expertise.

CAREER BYTE: TIPS FOR DISSEMINATION

When preparing to disseminate your work or expertise, there are several tips to consider that will increase your success. Whether you are a novice or a seasoned professional, reviewing strategies for dissemination like the following is always prudent:

- **You should be considered an expert on what you are disseminating:** The more knowledgeable you are, the greater the impact your voice will have on the audience.

- **Take every opportunity to disseminate, no matter how small:** You can join discussions on current issues in your areas of expertise in person, online, or in writing. The more your voice is heard on your selected topics, the more influence you impart.

- **Promote your expertise and work:** In essence, you need to be your own public relations or marketing firm. No one knows your work better than you do. Your voice is unique, so let others know in both the professional and public domains. This might mean submitting abstracts for poster or podium presentations, or writing query letters for journals of all types, or answering calls for articles. It could also mean posting links to your published work on social media or reporting other important accomplishments. (If you post a link to a publication of yours, be sure you follow any copyright guidelines set forth by the journal that published your work, if applicable.)

- **Use social media:** Interact with others on social media platforms within the context of your expertise/scope/practice. Don't just repost other people's content. Create your own posts that reflect your unique voice.

- **Challenge yourself:** Do not let previous experiences or rejection prevent you from using your voice.

- **Find a mentor:** If you are unsure as to the best way to disseminate in your written or verbal voice, find a mentor who can help you move this part of your career forward. Asking for guidance and direction is a positive action on your career path.

- **Always be prepared to disseminate:** Being prepared will enhance your chances of being heard. You never know when an opportunity will arise or be presented to you. Suppose you got an email right now asking you to submit an abstract or give a speech in two days. Could you do it?

> • **Create different versions of your abstract(s):** These should have different word and character counts, be geared toward different audiences, include different keywords, and be designed for different methods of dissemination, including journals, presentations, webinars, guest lectures, and opinion pieces.

USING YOUR VOICE FOR ADVOCACY THROUGH THE MEDIA

An *advocate* is an individual or group that provides support and encouragement. Advocates assist in getting a message across. They succinctly and effectively express their view or the view of someone else to people who need to hear that message.

Often, nurses advocate for themselves and for their patients or students. Less common is the nursing professional who speaks up on behalf of the nursing profession, either formally through an organization or informally on an individual basis. Often, other healthcare groups—for example, the American Medical Association—provide representatives to deliver quotes about healthcare issues, which the public sees in newspapers and other publications, in online posts, and on television. This occurred regularly during the COVID-19 pandemic. Nurses, however, are rarely quoted. With all the changes at the forefront of healthcare today, and with the increased prominence of nurses during the pandemic, now, more than ever, it is time for nurses—the largest group of healthcare providers globally—to have their voices heard.

In 1997, Sigma Theta Tau International (STTI) published the original "Woodhull Study on Nursing and the Media: Health Care's Invisible Partner." This study examined the extent to which nurses were used as sources by the print news media on stories related to healthcare issues. Overall, the study found that nurses represented only 4% of experts in sourced material (STTI, 1997). In essence, nurses were ignored as sources for health-related stories, and their voices went unheard in the public forum.

In 2018, the Woodhull Study (Mason et al.) was replicated to determine if any progress had been made over the last 20 years in the representation of nurses as sources in the media. Again, the study results were published by STTI. The overall finding was that little had changed since the original study was published in 1998. Nurses continued to be relatively absent as sources for the media when reporting on healthcare issues and stories, thus limiting their expert voices and perspectives in the public forum.

The researchers (Mason et al., 2018) similarly found that nurses continue to lack a voice in the media (although this does not make it any less frustrating for members of the nursing profession). They continue to attempt to address the potential causative reasons for this lack of representation, and that work will continue. All of us within the nursing profession should view their commitment to spearhead a discussion on this issue as a call to action to do all we can to ensure our voices are heard by journalists and the public.

As individuals, we should offer our voices as experts to media sites within our geographical area. Starting at this level can lead to opportunities on a larger platform, which will benefit the profession. Even increasing your presence on social media can enable you to break into the mainstream media. For example, one school nurse named Robin Cogan, MEd, RN, NCSN, also known as the Relentless School Nurse (https://www.relentlessschoolnurse.com), frequently posted on social media sites like Twitter about reopening schools during the pandemic. Because of her presence on social media and on her own website, CNN and other news media outlets reached out to her to serve as an expert on the subject in live interviews and news articles. This is movement in a positive direction for nurses' presence in the media, where our voices are needed. When our voices are left out of the discussion, there's a void in expertise that can't be filled by others.

CAREER BYTE: ADVOCATING FOR THE NURSING PROFESSION

Some examples of ways you can advocate for the nursing profession include:

- Writing an editorial for your local news outlet or a national news source

- Starting a blog to present your unique perspective and expertise

- Posting on social media (as discussed in Chapter 8)

- Exploring healthcare-related accounts on social media sites and joining in discussions that are relevant to you

This type of participation can be a first step to finding your voice as a champion for nursing.

USING YOUR VOICE IN PROFESSIONAL ORGANIZATIONS

An excellent place to find and grow your voice is through a professional organization. Being an active member in a professional organization—on a local level, statewide, regionally, nationally, or internationally—enables you to formulate your ideas and to present them in diverse ways. For example, you can share your expertise on committees and for projects associated with the organization and advocate for positions that are important to the organization's mission and goals. You can also use your voice in a professional organization to disseminate your work (e.g., at conferences hosted by the organization); to network; to mentor or be mentored; to give back through volunteerism; and to make a difference for the organization, its members, and the nursing profession as a whole. Remember: Nurses who are members of the International Council of Nurses began somewhere!

> *Note*
> Your willingness to participate in a professional organization and share your point of view and your expertise will be rewarded in more ways than you could ever imagine.

USING YOUR VOICE AS A POLITICAL ADVOCATE

Politics and policymaking are areas in which the voices of more nurses are needed and can make a significant impact. Becoming a political advocate enables you to actualize your influence on nursing and healthcare-related issues on a much larger platform. There are few nurses in political office in local, state, federal, and national government across the globe, and their numbers are disproportionate to the 20 million nurses in the workforce worldwide (World Health Organization, n.d.). But nurses can still be active in politics even if they are not in political office by becoming members of nursing organizations that influence policymaking at all levels.

To remind the public that nurses have diverse expertise on global health issues in all settings where people receive care and health education, we need to make our presence known. You, as an individual or as a member of a group, can do that by getting involved in a grassroots effort that relates to an issue in nursing or healthcare. Using our voices to stir up some noise can move an issue to the forefront that was not there before or bring attention to a need for input from nurses on a particular issue.

THE COVID-19 PANDEMIC TASK FORCE

An example of nurses using their voices to effect change occurred in the United States after the 2020 presidential election, when the new president formed a COVID-19 Pandemic Task Force that included no nurses. For weeks afterward, nurses of all varieties from around the country voiced their concern about the absence of nurses on the task force on social media platforms—particularly Twitter. Nurses were even nominating their colleagues to serve by posting and tagging the new president, the first lady, senators, and congressional representatives. While it's not clear whether this made an impact on the president, the fact is that a nurse *did* get put on that task force, giving nursing a seat at this particularly important political and healthcare table.

You can also engage in political advocacy by:

- Participating in a political campaign for a candidate who is interested in promoting or sponsoring legislation that relates to nursing and healthcare

- Running for political office yourself at any level—local, state, or federal

- Becoming actively involved in political or issues-related organizations that share the same vision that you do

USING YOUR VOICE TO NETWORK

Networking is a process by which an individual or group makes connections for a purpose. It can be an invaluable way to meet and interact with people who can assist you in your career, both in the short term and the long term. Networking can also be an excellent way to obtain information that will assist you as you move forward on your career path. The exchange of ideas that occurs during networking can even result in a positive impact on the overall profession.

> **Tip**
>
> Maintaining contact with individuals from diverse backgrounds can be very beneficial as you progress on your career path.

The following are some key characteristics of a network:

- At least two individuals participate.

- Participants have similar interests.

- Participants have desirable information or expertise.

- Participants have the ability and desire to learn through reciprocal communication.

- Participants have the ability to be heard and to listen.

- Participants are accessible via numerous communication channels in a global environment.

- Participants are committed to the networking process.

- Participants can communicate on a variety of diverse topics.

- Participants want to help others with their career paths and professional development.

A professional network is only as effective as its members—what they offer the network and how they use what the network has to offer them. For this reason, once you have established a professional network, it is critical that you nurture and maintain it. As you meet new individuals who might benefit from your professional network or who have expertise to add to it, establish relationships with them and invite them to join.

An effective way to develop a network is to share your contact information with people you want to add to your network and obtain theirs in return. While some individuals use business cards, you can also upload contact information to your phone or similar device. Just be sure to save it. You never know when someone in your network will be able to assist you with your career advancement!

You can communicate with members of your network in various ways—by email, text, direct message on social media platforms, and so on. By using these communication technologies, you can bridge different time zones and geographical locations, thus broadening the potential membership and expertise of your professional network.

CAREER BYTE: NETWORKING PITFALLS TO AVOID

While there are many advantages to networking, there are also some pitfalls you want to avoid. These include the following:

- **Don't allow any single participant's issues to become bigger than the network itself:** This can lead to a dysfunctional network that does not benefit anyone.

- **Do not offer expertise, assistance, or guidance if you cannot follow through on delivery:** Trust is crucial to the maintenance of a professional network.

- **Do not underuse participants of the network:** Every participant was included in the network for a reason, so make sure to use and value their expertise.

- **Keep network communications private within the group:** Sharing of information beyond the network should be mutually agreed upon by all participants.

- **Be careful what is posted on any social media site related to your professional network:** Remember that nothing is ever fully deleted from the internet.

- **Do not take any member of your professional network for granted:** Each participant gives their time and expertise, which should be acknowledged and appreciated.

FINAL THOUGHTS

Both your written and verbal voice will change over your career journey. With time and experience come confidence and presence, as well as a greater desire to use your voice to advance the nursing profession and your place within that profession.

You don't have to be the loudest or the boldest to have an impact. You don't have to be the most prolific writer or participate in every activity afforded to you. Your voice simply needs to be present within your comfort zone at each step of your career path—not inhibited by others or circumstances.

Challenge yourself to use your voice. Allow yourself to be imperfect and for your voice to be as well. Being imperfect is just as much of a learning experience as being a success. With each use of your voice, you will learn, reflect, and gain confidence in your voice. You have something to share—something to offer others in nursing and the larger healthcare arena—that is uniquely you. If you don't get that information out there, it may be lost to those who might benefit from it forever. You will know when you are ready, and it is your time to use your voice!

REFERENCES

Mason, D. J., Nixon, L., Glickstein, B., Han, S., Westphaln, K., & Carter, L. (2018). The Woodhull Study revisited: Nurses' representation in health news media 20 years later. *Journal of Nursing Scholarship*, *50*(6), 695–704. https://doi.org/10.1111/jnu.12429

Sigma Theta Tau International. (1997). *The Woodhull Study on nursing and the media: Health care's invisible partner*. Indianapolis, IN: Author. http://hdl.handle.net/10755/624124

World Health Organization. (n.d.). *Health workforce—data and statistics*. https://www.who.int/hrh/statistics/en/

10

ENTREPRENEURSHIP FOR THE PROFESSIONAL NURSE

"Starting a business is like anything else that is new and challenging: scary and all-consuming. The driving force inside of me was my passion and my excitement about what was ahead. It was that driving force that kept me moving forward. It has not been easy or stress-free, and no one should ever tell you it is, but it is fulfilling and rewarding. I have been doing this for 17 years now in my consulting business. I work more hours than I ever did before. I stress about things I never worried about before. Is it worth it? Absolutely. I love all the opportunities and challenges I have been afforded in this phase of my career. I love hard work and I now have it. It is all mine, and I can share it with those who want to benefit from my expertise. I am the manager of my career destiny."

–L. M., PhD, MN, RN

TAKING ON NEW CHALLENGES

As nurses enter new phases of their career, they are often interested in taking on new challenges, finding new growth opportunities, or supplementing their income due to changes in their personal and/or professional lives. Fortunately, as a nurse, you can use your skills, educational background, and expertise in a variety of settings, and many individuals can benefit from what you have to offer.

One way to broaden your impact is to start and run a business. In this way, nurses in clinical practice and advanced clinical practice—or in academic, administrative, research, or leadership positions, both inside and outside of nursing—can offer their knowledge and skills to a wider audience. This wider audience might include (to name a few):

- Other healthcare professionals

- Publishing companies

- Law firms

- Pharmaceutical companies

- Nursing organizations

> **Note**
>
> Your business can be informal or formal, small or large, full-time or part-time. No matter how you do it, selling a product—namely, your expertise—can be both fulfilling and profitable.

A SUCCESSFUL CLINICAL ENTREPRENEURIAL EXPERIENCE

"A group of five very dedicated and motivated women—nurses and health professionals—decided after working within diverse healthcare environments and related positions that it was time to 'get out of the boat' and to move forward with a concept and vision that was important to us and to the population we cared most about: medically fragile children. Through the efforts of us five women, our state legislators, and our friends—who believed in our dream and helped make it a reality—what began as a community-health school project focusing on a needs assessment in a

particular community turned into a not-for-profit corporation. The Pre-scribed Pediatric Extended Care (PPEC) facility opened in 2005. The original plan was to provide 24-hour care to medically fragile children, but we eventually accepted that providing 12-hour care was an improvement over providing no services at all.

"The process of opening the PPEC was arduous at times—raising aware-ness, raising money, making repeated trips to the state capitol to meet with people about licenses and reimbursement issues, and holding together the dream. We were lucky in that we had already established ourselves in our respective career positions, and we had security and support systems that allowed us to take that 'trip out of the boat' without fear. We had a community that held fundraisers and awareness events for people who could make a difference financially and politically. We had other healthcare professionals who backed our vision and mission and lent support in so many ways when needed. These supporters did not wait to be asked; they simply showed up and volunteered. Each of us had a skill set—a level of pediatric nursing, a financial background, community connections—that was a little different from the others, so as a team, we were more effective and more powerful than any one of us individually.

"The six-year time frame from the inception of the idea to the opening of the licensed PPEC was not without trials and tribulations, roadblocks due to money and to local and state regulations, facility location and zoning issues, and compromises that had to be made by all. The thread that held us all together to meet our mission was knowing that the need for care of medically fragile children was there, and it was 'our calling' to meet that need. We did, and we continue to do so.

"In the last three years, we have moved from a facility that housed 35 children to a facility that can accommodate 60 children. We have opened a second PPEC location, which can serve 30 more children, in another part of the state to meet the needs of a broader population. We provide comprehensive nursing, medical, and associated healthcare services to our children and their families and have successfully been doing so now for 16 years. We are making a difference, and we will continue our mis-sion to expand our services even further."

–S. K., MSN, BSN, APRN

OPPORTUNITIES FOR NURSE ENTREPRENEURS: A POTENTIAL FIT FOR EVERYONE

Nurses who are interested in an entrepreneurial career transition can travel several paths. For example, you can look for an opportunity that matches your current skill set and expertise. Or you can look for an opportunity in an area completely outside your experience, knowing that some educational advancement may accompany such a career move.

Here are a few ideas to consider if you are interested in striking out on your own:

- **Forensic nursing:** This might be a good fit for you if you have worked in an emergency department or a morgue, have knowledge or interest in police or detective work, or enjoy the process of solving puzzles.

- **Medical staffing:** Opening a medical staffing office might be an opportunity you wish to pursue if you have done staffing within a clinical agency and know the ins and outs of the business.

- **Medical reviews, quality improvement reviews, medical billing, or chart coding:** If you have done chart reviews during your career, you could seek out opportunities to review medical record reviews or quality improvement efforts, medical billing, or chart coding. You can perform these types of tasks working for an insurance company or within your own consulting business.

- **Legal consultation:** If you enjoy delving into the legal aspects of nursing and healthcare—for example, scope-of-practice issues, negligence, or similar—then consulting on malpractice or similar cases may be right for you. You can even do this as a full-time position on your own or get hired by a law firm.

- **Wellness coaching:** If you are an exercise guru or a proponent of self-care, consider putting those skills to use by becoming a wellness coach. You could serve in this capacity for a large corporation that has a wellness center, providing consulting services as well as hands-on training for others who work there. Alternatively, you could build a practice working with individuals. As more and more people become interested in self-care and preventive care, they are seeking out mindfulness training, meditation, yoga, and other physical and mental health strategies and interventions. Now is a great time to venture into such work.

- **Holistic care:** If you are an advanced practice nurse, you could develop a holistic care center, collaborating with other healthcare providers to offer self-care services and/or education for the general public or for certain client populations who have specific healthcare needs—for example, patients with diabetes, hypertension, anxiety, depression, and similar. (Be sure to look into obtaining third-party reimbursement for this type of work.)

- **Prenatal or birthing coach:** If you have been a maternity nurse, think about applying your skill set as an exercise coach for pregnant women or as an expert in a birthing center.

- **Mental health counseling:** If you are psychiatric/mental health nurse—especially if you are an advanced practice nurse—consider providing mental health counseling services to others. There has never been a greater need for nurses with this expertise to provide these types of services, as citizens around the globe are contending with so many physical, social, and economic issues. Just be sure you know your legal and ethical responsibilities!

- **Child services:** If pediatrics is your area of expertise, you could open a summer camp or an after-school program with the goal of encouraging kids to engage in physical activity and/or to address the various mental health issues that today's children are working through.

- **Consulting for school systems:** Working as a consultant for a school system in your area could be a good fit for you. This is an especially critical role at the moment due to the COVID-19 pandemic, as health and education experts attempt to determine how to safely reopen schools across the globe. You can implement your ideas as a consultant through a larger program or organization or as a business you develop on your own.

- **Designing nursing exams:** Are you a master educator with expertise in test construction, design, evaluation, and/or specific content for the various nursing and related certification examinations? There are many opportunities for this type of expertise—particularly for larger test companies and organizations that administer certification examinations—to work as a consultant for test development and evaluation. The marketplace continues to show evidence that there is a need for this type of work.

> **Note**
>
> Nurses should be the ones to design licensure and/or practice exams and review books for nurses because these exams are *for* nurses. In the past, much of this work was done by others, who did not necessarily have the expertise in either nursing or test development and evaluation—and it showed.

- **Developing healthcare-related software apps:** If you are a technological expert with an innovative and entrepreneurial spirit, you could be the one to develop the next big healthcare app used by clinicians, educators, data collectors and researchers, patients, students, and so on. Think about all the health issues you could help solve by creating an app or some other technological innovation! You can do this type of work on your own or as part of a larger technological company working in this area.

- **Medical writing or editing:** If you like to impart information to others, consider becoming a medical writer or editor for a nursing or healthcare-related organization, medical education company, or publishing house. Many consultants who do this type of work operate on a contract basis and charge by the hour or project on an escalating monetary scale, depending on their years of experience and their expertise. You could also consider working as a health reporter for a local newspaper or TV or radio station. To break into that industry, try writing a health education report on a timely topic, such as obesity prevention, and send it to those types of organizations.

- **Designing healthcare facilities:** Do you love architecture and design? Do you have experience or perhaps even an academic degree in art or architecture? If so, consider taking on a consultant role in healthcare environmental design for a company in your area that designs and builds healthcare facilities.

- **Translating or interpreting:** If you are multilingual, consider putting your language skills to use as a translator or interpreter. This can involve verbal communication, written communication, or both. In our diverse global environment, being able to speak and write in more than one language can benefit both you and the organization that uses your services. Given the demand for these services, this is a business with great growth potential, whether you operate as a consultant in-house or as a free-standing business.

Note

Whatever entrepreneurial avenue you choose, make it a point to market your expertise and knowledge as a professional registered nurse. Show your potential clients what you have to offer them that others do not because of what you have done in your career.

If none of these ideas resonates with you, try coming up with some of your own. Or implement one you've already thought of. Many of us have developed implementation plans during our career. Could one you've written be parlayed into a consultant role or business plan?

If becoming an entrepreneur is something you want to do, do not shy away from an idea that you think could make a difference for others. Don't say to yourself, "This idea is OK, but it will never happen. I'm not a businessperson." And don't be inhibited by the steps you might need to take. You never know what you can accomplish. If what you envision is something you are passionate about and believe can be impactful, do some research, seek advice, and see if there are similar ventures out there. Remember: Every single company whose products or services you use in your personal or professional life started out as an idea that someone took a chance on. Why not do the same?

Note

For more information on potential entrepreneurial opportunities for nurses, check out the National Nurses in Business Association (https://nnba.nursingnetwork.com/) and the Society of Nurse Scientists, Innovators, Entrepreneurs & Leaders (https://www.sonsiel.org/).

ONE OF THE MOST COMMON AND SUCCESSFUL NURSE ENTREPRENEURSHIPS: LEGAL CONSULTATION

"I began my work as a legal consultant and expert witness for a law firm more than 21 years ago, when nurses who chose law as a second profession were few and far between. I started off doing chart reviews for law cases involving nurses in my area who worked at institutions and agencies where I had no affiliation. A friend who was a lawyer recommended me to a malpractice attorney, and so my work as a legal consultant began. At first, I charged a minimal consultation fee, as I wanted to keep working for them. But the more work I did and the more cases the lawyers won based in some part on my work or expert testimony, the more my consultation fee grew. Now, charging $400 an hour seems completely reasonable and is not questioned by any law firm that uses my services. I work for many law firms now, and my services are well-known and respected. I now make a particularly good living on my law work alone, and that is what I am doing since my retirement a few years back. If I were earlier in my career, I would probably go back to law school to get my JD, but for me legal consultation as a doctorally prepared nurse is perfect."

–K. F., DNSc, RN

GETTING STARTED

Many nurses at various points in their careers find themselves wanting to leave their current position and take on the challenge of starting their own business. Making this move involves a lot of thought and preparation.

As a first step, you must decide whether you want your new business to be your full-time career or a position that augments your full-time position. This decision will assist you in determining the importance of the income you can potentially make, as well as the amount of security the position can provide.

Note

You should not view starting your own business as a means to a quick buck or as a way of removing yourself from a more structured work environment. You will quickly find that this endeavor requires more time and involves many more risks than a traditional job—especially if you are making a full-time career change!

Next, you need to identify what you have to sell, what makes your business product unique, and what you want your business to look like. Fortunately, there are many real-world resources to help you with all aspects of starting and successfully running a business. For example:

- Local and state business development centers

- Local chambers of commerce

- Local schools of business, including their centers for entrepreneurship or think tanks

Tip

Some academic institutions and other organizations sponsor business plan competitions. Often, the prize for winning is access to a seasoned mentor. For a list of these competitions, see https://www.comcapfactoring.com/blog/list-of-business-plan-competitions-by-state/.

In addition, there are loads of resources online. Here are a few websites to check out:

- The U.S. Small Business Association (https://www.sba.gov)

- The SBA Small Business Innovative Research (SBIR) and Small Business Technology Transfer (SBTT) programs (https://www.sbir.gov)

- *WSJ Business* (https://www.wsj.com/news/types/small-business)

- *Entrepreneur* (https://www.entrepreneur.com)

- Nursing organizations that provide mentors, such as Sigma Theta Tau International (https://www.sigmanursing.org/advance-elevate/careers/sigma-mentoring-cohort)

- The National Association for the Self-Employed (https://www.nase.org)

Finally, this page on the U.S. Bureau of Labor Statistics website offers information on the outlook for self-employed workers, broken down by industry: https://www.bls.gov/careeroutlook/2018/article/self-employment.htm.

You can also try searching the internet for opportunities that might be a good match for you. Just be sure they are reputable. There are many predatory companies looking to take your money and ruin your reputation, so be careful anytime you find something online that sounds too good to be true. Thoroughly investigate all ads, offers, or requests before you make any commitment or sign any contracts. Most importantly, do not give money or financial information to *anyone*.

Tip

Be sure that all internet sites to which you provide information related to your business or business opportunities are secure. The site address should begin with *https*, with the *s* indicating that the site is secure.

CHARTING YOUR CAREER: WORKING FROM HOME IS NOT THE SAME AS RUNNING A BUSINESS FROM HOME

The Bureau of Labor Statistics (https://www.bls.gov) counts self-employment in different ways. By one count, there were about 9.6 million self-employed workers in 2016. BLS predicts that this number will increase to 10.3 million by 2026. Many of these workers conduct their businesses from their homes.

Because of the COVID-19 pandemic, many workers (other than essential workers) transitioned from working on-site to working from home. Experts predict that many of these workers will want to continue working from home even after the pandemic is over.

If you have experience working for an employer from home, you should be aware that this is not quite the same as running your own business from your home. When you work for someone else, where you work should not affect your work responsibilities. You should keep the same hours and be available as if you were in your "real" office. The policies and procedures you work under are dictated by the company or organization you work for; they can't be changed based on what works for you at home. Thus, your workday should be conducted as if you were in a regular work environment.

If you are running your own business from your home, however, then *you* are the boss of your work environment, policies, and schedule. You are responsible only to you and to your clients. You must meet your committed project dates, but when you work on them is up to you. You can maintain a workday that reflects your needs and commitments. If you prefer to work later in the day or evening, then that can work for you. If you need to make calls or have virtual meetings, you can work more traditional hours on one or two days; then, the rest of your days, including the weekends, are for you to focus on the work you have taken on.

As an example, I have many projects that have deadlines—some for profit, and others as a volunteer. I treat them equally, as it is my business, and I can give them equal importance. I do not have to ask anyone when and where to spend my time as long as I meet my deadlines. I work during traditional business hours when I need to, but I also work late at night and sometimes very early in the morning. I work most weekends on my tutoring, as it fits into my schedule best then. I am free to work when it is best for me and my professional and personal responsibilities. That is an advantage of working from home for my own business versus working from home for someone else.

Finally, there are several videoconferencing tools available online that you can use to work from home alone or with your team. These include the following:

- Zoom
- Microsoft Teams
- Webex
- Skype
- Google Meet

Tip

If you are looking for such entrepreneurial opportunities outside of North America, check the equivalent types of organizations or websites for information that is relevant to the country where you want to start and build your business. And remember, being entrepreneurial often is limited by country norms, cultural expectations, and legal requirements for owning and running a business. Be sure you exercise your due diligence in researching all these areas at the initial stages of this process.

IMPORTANT CONSIDERATIONS

"After more than 25 years in academics, my career path changed. I left academics to pursue new opportunities as a nurse education consultant. Within all my excitement, I had qualms about being my own boss from a time perspective, a 'how to do this' perspective, and a financial perspective, just to mention a few. It was important for me not to question my decision when I was anxious or worried. In fact, that was the motivation to keep me moving forward. Using and finding my 'voice' outside of the academic world was initially scary and somewhat hard but then invigorating and fulfilling. Now it is the essence of what I do."

–L. M., PhD, MN, RN

If you have decided that you are ready for entrepreneurship, whether on a full-time or part-time basis, you may need to consider a variety of factors. These include the following:

- Finances

- Health insurance

- Workload

- Advertising and marketing

- Personnel

ABCS OF A SUCCESSFUL ENTREPRENEUR

A   Attention to detail and assiduousness

B   Belief in oneself

C   Contemplative and communicative

D   Driven and determined

E   Expertise to share

F   Follow-through

FINANCES

When people ponder stepping outside the traditional workforce, financial issues are often at the top of their list of concerns. Specifically, they wonder how much they should charge and how they should handle paying taxes.

Tip

When it comes to money, take the long view. Don't be so fixated on what to charge for your work in the short term that you dissuade clients from using your services in the long term!

When determining your fee structure, be somewhat flexible—particularly during the initial stages of your new venture. The idea during this phase is to build your clientele and establish your reputation. Often, this might mean taking less upfront so you can grow your business over time. That being said, don't let others take advantage of you. Know your worth!

As for taxes, here are a few points to keep in mind, assuming you live in and are filing taxes in the United States:

- If you will be working as an independent contractor, you need to fill out a W-9 form and, in most cases, pay your own taxes—usually on a quarterly, rather than yearly, basis.

- Some money from each paycheck will need to go to the IRS. Don't spend it all!

- If you are opening a small business and you are the only employee, you will have to pay your own taxes on earned income.

- Have a separate bank account for your business, and use that account for business expenses and to pay taxes.

- If you are working from home or a stand-alone office, hire an accountant to help you itemize work-related purchases that you can deduct from your taxable income, such as computers and accessories, cellphones, office supplies, and travel expenses, including gas mileage (if you travel to see clients).

- An accountant is a critical key to your success. It is money well spent and will help you avoid issues down the line.

Tip

Every country has a different system for taxation, and each state or province within a country may levy additional taxes.

CHARTING YOUR CAREER: TO INCORPORATE OR NOT TO INCORPORATE

If you are starting a small business, it is important to consider whether you want to be incorporated. Incorporation has implications for taxes, insurance, liability, and more. Refer to the resources outlined in the "Getting Started" section earlier in this chapter for more information on the pros and cons of incorporation. You should also discuss this topic with your accountant and/or lawyer.

HEALTH INSURANCE

If you are planning to become self-employed on a part-time basis while continuing to work in your full-time position, health insurance is usually not an issue; in most cases, your insurance will continue through your employer. But if you are planning to leave your full-time position to become self-employed on either a part-time or full-time basis, you must consider how you will obtain and pay for health insurance.

Of course, if your spouse receives health insurance through an employer, then they may be able to simply add you to their policy. If not, you will have to purchase your own policy—and possibly purchase policies for any employees you hire. Purchasing your own health insurance policy takes time, research, and money out of your own pocket or profits.

> **Tip**
> Don't take health insurance and other benefits lightly. It is a good idea to know what options you have and how much they cost before making the decision to become self-employed.

WORKLOAD

Often, people decide to become self-employed or start their own small business with the notion that they will be in control of their time and will therefore have more time for other activities. In reality, entrepreneurs often find that the opposite is true.

In theory, you control what projects you agree to do, when they are due, how many projects you are responsible for at any one time, and how you structure your workdays. In practice, though, projects often grow beyond their initial scope, due dates change, projects overlap, and workdays often bleed into work nights and weekends.

> **Tip**
> Meeting deadlines for projects, arriving on time for appointments and meetings, promptly returning phone calls, and following up in a timely manner are essential to earning the trust of your clients and ensuring the success of your business.

The adage "Don't bite off more than you can chew" is particularly relevant for the self-employed individual!

ADVERTISING AND MARKETING

"In the beginning, I felt challenged as to how to take my expertise in nursing education and market it so others, particularly novice educators, could learn and benefit from what I had to offer. I thought about my network of colleagues, peers, and mentors who could assist me as I moved onto this new path. I got the word out to others about my interests and my career path change. I volunteered for projects and committees within organizations to 'market' my skills and expertise. I took on small projects with companies that I knew would beget bigger projects, and they did. I marketed my NCLEX review and tutoring locally and, over time, word-of-mouth about my clients' successes increased my client base and eventually expanded my review to schools and colleges of nursing across the country. Their students' successes begat other schools inquiring about my services and hiring me. Over the past years, my portfolio has expanded to diverse and varied projects and clients. My successes and my work ethic led others to want to work with me. My volunteerism led to more of the work I loved and some paying gigs as well. My willingness to learn new things, challenge myself and others, and enthusiastically take on projects has led to more work with individuals, groups, and organizations that I value and love to contribute to. Social media has certainly played an important role in advertising and marketing. With daily posts for specific audiences, with well-thought-out comments on posts from other audiences within nursing and healthcare, and from responding to calls for assistance or my particular areas of expertise, my

clientele and reach have grown. For a self-owned busi-
ness, the more advertising and marketing you can obtain
at minimal to no cost, the better for your bottom line as a
business owner."

–L. M., PhD, MN, RN

Even if you are a one-person operation, getting the word out about
your offerings is critical to building a business that will grow and last.
Here are a few ways to achieve advertising and marketing success:

- Let your clients sell your work and your successes through word-
of-mouth.

- Network with individuals who can assist you with promoting
your work.

- Build your own website, create a blog, and/or maintain a social
media presence.

- Publish in local print or online newspapers, depending on your
clientele.

- Advertise in professional organizations' journals and on their
websites.

- Advertise in other publications or on websites that market to your
prospective clientele.

- Attend conferences to network, market yourself and your business, and perhaps even exhibit (when your budget allows).

Cost is a factor with advertising and marketing. When thinking about
the most effective means to get the word out about yourself and your
business, you will want to keep cost in mind. A 30-second commercial during the Super Bowl would certainly enable you to spread your
message to a wide audience, but it probably would not be the most
cost-effective approach! (Well, unless you have $5.6 million, which was
the average advertising cost for a 30-second commercial for the 2021
Super Bowl.)

As mentioned, one way to market your business is by creating a website. For many potential clients, this website will serve as the face of your business. If you lack the necessary expertise to build a professional-looking site, consider hiring someone to build it for you. It will cost you, but it's worth the investment!

An important part of your website is your web address, or URL. It should reflect the name of your business in some way. To search for available URLs, check reputable sites such as https://www.godaddy.com/domain or https://domains.google/. If you find that someone has used the URL you wanted, don't get frustrated; be flexible and creative when choosing your URL.

Know the market in which you want to sell your skills, knowledge, or product. Also, define your niche. Take what is unique and special about your expertise and market that. Don't try to be like everyone else; be your most authentic and unique self in your career.

CHARTING YOUR CAREER: NAMING YOUR BUSINESS

The name of your business can be a powerful marketing tool, conveying to prospective customers what kind of work you do and what level of service they can expect. Be aware, though, that as with URLs, the name you choose for your business may or may not be available for your use. For help determining whether the name you choose for your business is in fact available for use, refer to the list of resources in the "Getting Started" section earlier in this chapter. Alternatively, seek help from a qualified attorney.

PERSONNEL

Even if you are starting your business as a one-person affair, a time may come when you need to hire additional staff. What type of staff and how many people you need will depend on your desire for growth, your current and projected workload, your budget, and the marketplace. The resources offered earlier in this chapter can provide you with information about dealing with personnel issues in a small business.

PERSEVERANCE AS A MEANS TO ENTREPRENEURIAL SUCCESS

"I had thought for a long time about making a change in my career. I had been a chemotherapy infusion nurse for many years in an acute care setting. I often did some home health cases providing infusion therapy in patients' homes and found the experience of being outside the confines of the hospital walls and structure to be enticing. I decided to 'moonlight' more often for an infusion-therapy company. Eventually I left my full-time position in the acute care setting to perform infusion therapy in patients' homes full time, with the hope of one day creating my own similar business. I wanted to be my own boss, set my own hours, train my own staff to provide care that I believed was of the highest quality, and do all of this while making a good living for myself and my staff. Over the next two years, I developed my version of a business plan, examined the marketplace, spoke to physicians and nurse practitioners I knew who I thought would refer patients to me, and researched reimbursement and liability.

"I thought the idea was sound. Although I had good intentions for serving home-care patients who required infusion therapy, I found that the timing wasn't right. There were many infusion-therapy companies—some associated with established home care agencies, some affiliated with hospitals and insurance companies, and some that were free-standing but had longevity. I was discouraged but not down. I decided to keep looking for my niche.

"I researched to find a market that was not being served or not being served widely, and then I tapped into that area. It was in a more rural area and not close to my current location, so I thought if I wanted to make this work, I would have to move. I knew I could make a difference and make a living, as evidenced by the other companies out there, so I took a leap of faith and, armed with the confidence I had in myself to be successful, I moved.

"I worked over a three-year period for a home health agency as I did all the necessary work to create my own infusion business. I leaned on friends and mentors and experts in how to be successful at this venture. I went back to school and completed my master's degree and was certified as a nurse

practitioner. I took continuing education courses related to infusion therapy to maintain my relevancy and currency with all the up-to-date management and interventional strategies.

"For the last seven years I have been the owner of my own infusion-therapy company, providing this necessary service to patients just as I always wanted to do. I started small and have grown, but not so much that I couldn't handle it. While I am proud of my perseverance and my drive, I am most proud of the fact that I didn't give up and accomplished my career goal. I knew this is what I was meant to do, and now I get to do it every day. So, what started off as a difficult experience turned out to be the best experience of my nursing career."

–M. B., MSN, BSN, ARNP

11

WORK-LIFE BALANCE ISSUES: MANAGING PERSONAL AND PROFESSIONAL TIME

"I have no work-life balance since March of 2020 when the pandemic began. Working in practice is more days in a row than I could have imagined in February of 2020. Work does not end when I leave the hospital, as I need to then come home, strip in my garage, shower not once but twice, and then sleep and start again. My support system is not present physically, as I have my husband and 4-year-old living with my in-laws. I work in the COVID-19 ICU, and most of the patients have died. I didn't want to expose my family to what I was exposed to; thus, they are not here. I try and find little things to do to relax me, but I can't. There is no balance for me or my colleagues. There is just work."

–D. A., BSN, CCRN

*"I am constantly asking myself, when will I get a break?
I don't really have a relaxing personality, but I do love to
watch movies when I can stay awake and am not working. I have limited time when I am not working, even
more since the pandemic. Working from home is now a
24-hour, seven-days-a-week job. I worked from home
before the pandemic, but now everyone is working from
home, and emails, texts, and phone calls are coming earlier in the morning and later at night. My excuse to myself
is, what else do I have to do but work? There is nothing
to do and nowhere to go. But I do feel my stress levels
going up, and I don't sleep well. My friends have given
me suggestions as to how to relax, how to find balance in
my life. The response to them and to myself is, 'OK, after
this project is done,' or, 'That's really not for me.' Will
I ever achieve the balance in my life that so many of my
friends and colleagues have, or am I just wired this way?"*

–M. S., DNSc, RN

WORK-LIFE BALANCE: THE DILEMMA

If you are reading this chapter and asking yourself, "What does balance
have to do with my work and life?" then this chapter is specifically
written for you (and me). We all grapple with how to maintain some
semblance of balance in our lives, with all the juggling we do each day.
While each of us has our own responsibilities, family, work, school, life
issues, and unexpected incidents, not all of us manage everything in our
lives in a healthy way—at least not all the time.

Nursing professionals know about the health-illness continuum. We
understand how the body responds to stress and why it is important
to find a balance between work and life. It is in the best interest of our
physiological and mental health to find the balance that works best for
us to live and work with minimal stress. The old saying "all work and

no play" is not just a colloquialism; it is a lesson to be learned for our own well-being.

WORK-LIFE BALANCE: OUR REALITY OF LITTLE TO NONE . . .

Nurses generally live in two quite different worlds. Our professional world usually revolves around caring and doing for others, whether through patient care or in one of the diverse nursing positions in which we contribute to the overall profession but do not directly manage patients. These could be positions in academics, research, politics and policy-making, consultation, administration, and so many more. In all these positions, nurses often put the needs of their patients, students, and clients first—in other words, ahead of their own needs and wants.

By their very nature, nursing professionals are caring individuals. This can be manifested in managing patient care as well as in meeting deadlines, completing projects, teaching a full credit load of classes, and so on. When the demands of our professional life interfere with the demands of our personal life, an imbalance inevitably ensues. This imbalance might be evident through physical and mental health symptoms as well as professional or personal burnout.

> **Note**
> This imbalance has never been more evident than during the COVID-19 pandemic—although imbalances were present before March 2020 and will remain long after the pandemic is over.

Because nurses in all positions have responsibilities that require them to be at the top of their game, it is incumbent on each of us to at least consider how we can find balance in our professional and personal lives. Work-life balance does not have to be evenly divided. There will be times when your professional life consumes 75% of your time and your personal life gets 25% of your attention. There will be other times when those percentages vary—and perhaps even flip. And while we might think we can divide ourselves into two pieces, we can't. This reality is often difficult for us to acknowledge. But the truth is that if we, as nursing professionals, do not take care of ourselves, our physical and mental exhaustion will begin to take its toll. Exhaustion, frustration, and stress can lead to poor concentration, mistakes, burnout, and total dissatisfaction in both parts of our one life. Remember: We can care for others only as effectively as we care for ourselves.

THE CURRENT ENVIRONMENT

The general movement nationally and internationally has been toward finding a reasonable, tolerable, and acceptable means of balancing our lives—not just for nursing professionals, but for everyone in the workforce. Individuals need to commit to themselves and find what works best for them in terms of striking a balance between their personal and professional selves within the cultural expectations and norms in which each of us lives.

There are several publications, national initiatives, apps, blogs, help lines, and other resources to help individuals find balance. There are also coaches and experts in meditation, mindfulness, yoga, and other self-care interventions. The bottom line is that you have to find what works best for you—even if it is not mainstream or the current fad. Maybe swimming, or walking, or driving, or even building things helps you feel centered and grounded when you are overworked and stressed. Self-care and finding work-life balance is about you and no one else. Now is the time to see if you can find balance for yourself.

> **Note**
>
> You might not be able to do the things that help you stay balanced every day. That's OK. For many of us, baby steps are the way to start. What's important is that you make an effort to move toward a healthier way of living.

TIPS AND STRATEGIES TO ACHIEVE WORK-LIFE BALANCE

You can use several tips and strategies in your efforts to achieve work-life balance. But first, you must do an honest and complete self-assessment of both your professional and personal lives. What are your commitments at home and at work that can't be changed? What can you modify in the way of time and/or responsibility? What can you delegate to others? Think of the answers to these questions as your personal and professional priority list.

Once you have completed your self-assessment, make a commitment to yourself to engage in self-care measures. Here are a few places to start:

- **Get enough sleep:** Stick to a sleep routine both on the days that you work and on your days off. To achieve this, try shutting off all electronic devices one hour earlier than you normally would. This is a small step but one in a positive direction.

- **Eat right:** Eat healthy foods on a regular basis—especially when you are not working. At work, things inevitably get in the way, which becomes your good excuse to slip.

- **Be sure you are moving:** Notice that I did not say "Be sure you are exercising," which for some of you evokes visions of sweaty gyms and intimidating equipment. Moving can be walking, hiking, swimming, biking, or just simply moving around in your house. For example, if you live in a house with stairs, walk up and down them two or three times every hour. Remember: Small steps can make a big difference.

> **Note**
> The main obstacle to taking self-care measures is *you*. So, just this once, make a commitment to yourself.

Think about what other types of self-care activities might be of interest to you in your efforts to seek balance. Ask your friends and colleagues how they find their moments of Zen. Also think back to earlier times in your own life. Are there things you used to enjoy doing that relaxed you—say, playing a musical instrument, listening to music, watching movies, playing cards, or simply reading a book?

These days, in the aftermath of the pandemic, there are lots of self-care activities you can do in the privacy of your own home—for example, yoga classes, meditation classes, and training programs using a tread-mill or stationary bike. If these are not in your budget, simply make up your own activity. Maybe try using a calming or meditation app or relaxing in low lighting with soft music or sounds. There is so much for you to choose from.

> *Note*
> Remember, the worst thing that can happen is you try an activity and do not like it. In that case, just try something else or say now is not the time for you. If you choose the latter, though, make an appointment with your-self to try again in one month—and mark it on your calendar.

Asking for help is another way to find balance. However, this option is often overlooked. Many of us don't like to admit we sometimes could use help from our families, our friends, and other professionals. But we all feel overwhelmed at times—like our responsibilities at work and at home are more than we can handle effectively and efficiently. It is at these times that we must let go of our "I can do it all" attitude and ask for help. This might mean delegating whenever you can, both at work and at home. At work, discuss with your colleagues and peers how to redivide some of your work, at least for a short time. At home, ask your partner, your children, or other family members to help pick up any slack, whether that means cooking, clean-ing, doing laundry, driving the kids to after-school activities, or doing any of the other tasks that take up so much of your time.

> *Note*
> To use a sports metaphor, think of this as a short time-out, or as handing the ball to someone else just for a little while, so you can do some-thing just for you.

You should also practice effective time management—not just at work, but at home, too. Nurses tend to be effective at time management at work but not necessarily in their personal lives. And often, when we get behind, it's our self-care activities that fall off our to-do list. But if you can juggle all the things you are responsible for at work, you can use those same time-management skills in your personal life. One way to do this is to make a personal schedule, similar to how you make schedules at work, be they for managing patient care, leading a unit, or teaching nursing students for a semester. Just as you plan out your workdays, plan your time *outside* of work, making sure you have time to do whatever you need to do for you. I know, you're probably thinking, "That sounds good in theory, but it doesn't often work well in practice." But try it for a week and see how it goes. You can always reevaluate and modify—just like you do at work.

It's also important to learn to say no, which, for many of us, is not a word in our vocabulary. For some of us, saying no means we have been defeated or can't meet other people's expectations of us. But sometimes, a no to someone else means a yes to us, and that is a good thing. There is no bad karma associated with turning down an extra assignment or project. No one should think less of you if you honestly need a mental health day or even a half day, and if they do, well, there is nothing you can do about it. When you are overwhelmed to the point that not another thing will fit into your schedule, don't try to make things work just to make someone else's professional or personal life better. For once, think of yourself, and what *you* need.

Lastly, give yourself permission to achieve work-life balance. It is OK to take 30 minutes to decompress—from work and from home. I understand that this is not always possible, but again, start with small steps and work your way up. Remember: There is no perfect plan to achieve work-life balance. The important thing is the result: the ability to be healthy in all areas of your life.

Of course, tips and strategies to assist you in achieving work-life balance are only effective if you are willing and commit to trying them. It's easy to say you will do something that you know is good for you, but if you never commit to doing it for more than one day, you will have a difficult time reaching a balanced state. Remember: If others can do it, you can, too. Your professional and personal lives will thank you.

PARTING PERSONAL WORDS . . .

Those of you who know me personally know I am not the best example of someone with work-life balance. But I try. And if I fail, I try again.

I do different things to destress. Sometimes it is the littlest thing that works the best—like playing solitaire on my iPad to get out of my own head. But when all else fails, and I *really* need a balance reset, I take my myself to a hotel in a Disney location—whether it's Disneyworld or a Disney park somewhere else. Often, I work during the day and then go have fun in the park at night. There, I can just be me, with no expectations, no responsibilities, and no time schedule. This rejuvenates me and makes me happy and calm. It's my own little piece of work-life balance.

I'm not saying you have to do what I do. (I get it—not everyone loves Disney!) The point is, find *your* thing—the thing that restores and rejuvenates you. Then, go do it.

EXAMPLES OF NEW AND EXPERIENCED NURSE RESUMÉS

Lauren Kendall

1741 S. W. 93 Court, Miami, FL, 33156

(786) 221-4211; Email: lkendall@gmail.com

OBJECTIVE STATEMENT

To obtain an RN position in a pediatric oncology unit where I can utilize my formal nursing education and my personal experience as a survivor of pediatric cancer.

LICENSURE AND CERTIFICATION

FL RN License# 9915624	April 30, 2021–April 30, 2023
PALS Certification# 9821209	May 15, 2021–May 15, 2023
AHA BLS Certification# 44876	January 20, 2021–January 20, 2022

EDUCATION

Bachelor of Science in Nursing   August 18, 2018–May 9, 2021

Emory University School of Nursing, Atlanta, GA

    Magna Cum Laude, GPA 3.9

CLINICAL EXPERIENCE

Emory University Hospitals, Atlanta, GA   January 21, 2021–April 24, 2021

    Clinical Preceptorship, Pediatric Oncology

    Functioned as RN under the supervision of an RN preceptor, providing comprehensive care to

     children and families experiencing oncology health alterations and management.

WORK EXPERIENCE

Joe Dimagio Children's Hospital, Ft. Lauderdale, FL   May 1, 2018–December 31, 2020

    Float Ward Secretary, Pediatrics

HONORS AND AWARDS

Sigma Theta Tau International Honor Society of Nursing   April 15, 2021–Current

    Alpha Epsilon, Emory University, Atlanta, GA

Outstanding Clinical Award, Emory University, Atlanta GA   May 5, 2021

PROFESSIONAL ORGANIZATIONS

Member, National Student Nurses Association   September 1, 2019–May 9, 2021

Member, Georgia Association of Nursing Students   September 1, 2019–May 9, 2021

SPECIAL SKILLS

Bilingual, English/Spanish, Verbal and Written

Familiarity with Epic and PointClickCare Software

FIGURE A.1   Recent BSN graduate nurse resumé.

Kyle Looksie MPH, BSN, RN, CNRN

1111 Mission Road
Atlanta, GA 30253

404.825.4856
kylel @gmail.com

Education

Emory University Rollins School of Public Health, Atlanta, GA   December 2016
Master of Public Health

Harding University Carr College of Nursing, Searcy, AR   May 2011
Bachelor of Science, Nursing

Licensure/Certifications

Registered Nurse   Expires January 31, 2022

Certified Neuroscience Registered Nurse   Expires December 31, 2025

Advanced Cardiovascular Life Support   Expires June 2023

CPR and Basic Life Support   Expires June 2023

NIMS (National Incident Management System)   January 2013

Trauma Nursing Core Course   Expired November 2017

Work Experience

Emory University Hospital – Clifton Campus, Atlanta, GA   February 2017-Present
Unit Charge Nurse (Neurosurgical ICU)
- Plans, coordinates, and directs the daily operations of the unit
- Supervises staff and facilitates communication with physicians and internal administrators
- Addresses escalated issues amongst patients, families, and staff

Emory University Hospital – Clifton Campus, Atlanta, GA   September 2014-February 2017
Registered Nurse (Neurosurgical ICU)
- Incorporated knowledge of the nursing process and the professional standards of nursing in daily practice
- Applied knowledge and understanding of critically acute disease processes to perform detailed assignments/interventions
- Provided care based on the changing physical and psychosocial needs unique to the critical, neurologically impaired patient

St. Vincent Infirmary Medical Center, Little Rock, AR   June 2011-August 2014
Registered Nurse (Neurosurgical ICU and Neurosurgery Step-Down)
- Incorporated knowledge of the nursing process and the professional standards of nursing in daily practice
- Applied knowledge and understanding of critically acute disease processes to perform detailed assignments/interventions
- Provided care based on the changing physical and psychosocial needs unique to the critical, neurologically impaired patient

Harding University Carr College of Nursing, Searcy, AR   August 2012-May 2014
Clinical Associate (Advanced Med/Surg Course – VA Hospital, Little Rock, AR)
- Helped students to enhance their knowledge and use of evidence-based practice to care for patients in the ICU
- Assisted students to develop the critical thinking skills necessary for meeting the needs of the critically ill patient
- Evaluated student's performance using objective and subjective data

continues

FIGURE A.2 Experienced nurse resumé.

continued

Volunteer Experience/Observation
STTI Virtual Mini-Academy: Tools for Advancing Your Career Program   January 2021-April 2021
Presenter and Mentor
  ☒ Collaborates and presents on CV/resumé building, portfolios, and interviewing techniques
  ☒ Provides individualized mentoring and guidance for nurses wanting to advance their career

Coweta Samaritan Clinic, Newnan, GA   September 2016-July 2018
Volunteer Nurse and Public Health Practitioner

Christian Health Ministries, Searcy, AR   June 2011-May 2014
Volunteer Nurse

Arkansas Nursing Students' Association, Little Rock, AR   October 2011-October 2013
State Consultant
  ☒ Guided students toward creating a strategic plan and achieving organizational goals
  ☒ Advised and assisted students with annual convention planning
  ☒ Collaborated with faculty advisors throughout the state to improve student membership and compliance

Shenandoah East, West Point, AR   August 2009-June 2011
Arkansas Volunteer Ombudsman

Hospice Home Care   December 2005-May 2007
Volunteer

Honors and Awards
  ☒ Nominee for the Sister Teresa Joseph Babcock Award for Service Excellence, St. Vincent Infirmary, 10/2013
  ☒ ANCC Magnet Appraiser Escort, St. Vincent Infirmary, 12/2012
  ☒ Outstanding Community Service Award, Harding University Carr College of Nursing, 5/2011
  ☒ Daedalus Award, Harding University Carr College of Nursing, 5/2011
  ☒ NSNA Leadership U Award, National Student Nurses' Association, 5/2011
  ☒ First Student Board Member, Arkansas Nursing Foundation, 7/2010-7/2011
  ☒ Brian A. Sanders Scholarship, Harding University, 2009
  ☒ Academic Scholarship, Harding University, 2005-2009

Professional Organizations
  ☒ Sigma Theta Tau International, 10/2012-Present
  ☒ American Association of Neuroscience Nurses, 9/2012-Present
  ☒ American Nurses Association, 7/2011-Present
  ☒ National Student Nurses' Association, 8/2005-1/2015
      ☒ Sustaining Member, 1/2012-1/2015
      ☒ Member, 8/2005-10/2011
  ☒ Arkansas Nurses Association, 7/2011-8/2014
  ☒ Arkansas Nurses Foundation, 7/2010-12/2011
      ☒ Board Member, 7/2010-12/2011
  ☒ Arkansas Nursing Students' Association, 2005-8/2014
      ☒ Consultant to the Board of Directors, 10/2011-10/2013
      ☒ Legislative Chair, 10/2010-10/2011
      ☒ Legislative Chair & Nominations and Elections Chair, 10/2009-10/2010
  ☒ Harding University Nursing Students' Association, 2005-2011

FIGURE A.2 Experienced nurse resumé.

Publications
- *Coweta Samaritan Clinic 2016 Community Needs Assessment*, 12/2016
- *Cheryl Schmidt: The Nurse, Educator, and Mentor*, Arkansas Nursing News, Summer 2013 (Vol. 9, No. 3)
- Creator of the International Economic and Human Development Degree, Harding University, 5/2011
- The Implementation of Comprehensive School-Based Health Centers, National Student Nurses' Association, 4/2011
- *This Little Light of Mine, I'm Gonna' Let it Shine*, Harding Nursing Student Association's *The Pulse* and Harding University's Student Publication *The Bison*, 3/2011
- Increasing the Amount of Healthy Food Options and Providing for More Informed Choices in Health Care Facilities, National Student Nurses' Association, 4/2010
- *Debriding the Wound*, Harding Nursing Student Association's *The Pulse*, 4/2010
- *Relaying the Right Message*, Harding Nursing Student Association's *The Pulse*, 10/2010

Presentations
- Mentoring Cohort Panel, Sigma Theta Tau International, 5/2021
- Coweta Samaritan Clinic 2016 Community Needs Assessment, Coweta Samaritan Clinic, 11/2016
- Nonviolent Communication, Emory University Hospital, 5/2015
- Horizontal Violence and Nonviolent Communication, St. Vincent Infirmary Medical Center, 3/2012
- The Power of Resolution, Arkansas Nursing Students' Association Annual State Convention, 10/2011
- The Power of Resolution, Arkansas Nursing Students' Association Council of State Presidents, 3/2011
- Preventing Child Abuse Using Educational Material During Parent-Teacher Conferences, Harding University Carr College of Nursing, 12/2010
- Resolve for Resolution! – Everything You Wanted to Know About the Resolution Process…and More!, Arkansas Nursing Students' Association Annual State Convention, 10/2010
- Everything You Ever Wanted to Know About the Resolution Process…And More!, Arkansas Nursing Students' Association Council of State Presidents, 3/2010
- What is Public Health?, Harding Nursing Student Association, 10/2009

FIGURE A.2 Experienced nurse resumé.

B

CURRICULUM VITAE

CURRICULUM VITAE
LOIS S. MARSHALL, PHD, MN, RN
FEBRUARY 2021

- **Doctor of Philosophy,** University of Miami, School of Education, Coral Gables, FL, May 1999.
- **Master of Nursing,** Emory University, School of Nursing, Atlanta, GA, August 1980.
- **Bachelor of Science in Nursing,** University of Miami, School of Nursing, Coral Gables, FL, May 1978.

LICENSURE AND CERTIFICATION

- Registered Nurse License, Florida, #1013972
  Original License September 1978
  Current License April 2019 to April 2021

- Certified Pediatric Nurse (CPN), #20000378
  National Certification Board of Pediatric Nurse Practitioners
  and Nurses   2000-2005

PROFESSIONAL EXPERIENCE

- LSM Educational Consulting, Miami, FL   07/2004-Current
  - Principal and Owner
  - Consultative services to individuals, schools and colleges of nursing, professional organizations, for-profit companies
  - Consultative services include, but not limited to:
    - NCLEX®-RN/PN preparation for individual and groups of students within or outside of schools and colleges of nursing

- Faculty development related to instruction, curriculum design and implementation, curriculum and program evaluation; NCLEX® preparation of students, test design and evaluation
- Evidence-Based Nursing Practice
- Abstract Development
- Small Grant Writing and Research Development
- Scholarly Writing Development
- Career Development and Advancement
- Mentorship
- Project Management
- Marshall's NCLEX-RN Review, Group/Private Tutor 06/2004-Current
  - Developer/Presenter of Content/Strategies for over 300 individuals from United States and up to 5 countries
  - Developer/Presenter of Content/Strategies, 2-3 day review ongoing basis for more than 20 Schools/Colleges of Nursing within United States with more than 1,500 students total.
- Elsevier, ClinicalKey for Nurses, Philadelphia, PA 05/2007-Current
  - Consultant and Clinical Editor, Evidence-Based Nursing Monographs
  - Co-creator of Evidence-Based Nursing Monographs product from inception to current
  - Develop, maintain, and advance topic list for research-based monographs that are designed for practicing nurses at the bedside (hospital and home-based). Each monograph provides synopsis of most relevant and timely nursing research and other health-related research. Evidence-based recommendations are provided based on current practice and evidence provided in synopses.
  - Edit new and updated evidence-based nursing monographs. (currently 100 titles)

- Develop and work with new writers to advance their writing abilities for research monograph format.
- Adapt and add to monograph topic list based on current practice issues, including COVID-19.
- Internal and client-based presentations of evidence-based nursing in practice via webinars.
- Adaptation of Core Measures/Quality Indicators within Evidence-Based Nursing Monograph titles and format (since 2015).
- Lead, New Nurse Graduate Retention Program 2017
- International Association of Clinical Research Nurses 06/2019-Current
  - Project Manager
    - Directing and managing publication of professional organization's Core Curriculum via Kindle Digital Publishing (KDP).
  - Working with editors of publication, authors of chapters, and copyeditor for entire project.
  - Galen University School of Nursing   01/2015-04/2015
    - Part-Time On-Line Faculty, Pathophysiology
  - International Honor Society of Nursing, Sigma Theta Tau
    - Nurse Researcher Scholar in Residence   2005-2009
  - University of Miami, School of Nursing, Miami, FL 08/1980-08/2004
- Associate Professor of Clinical Nursing   07/2004-08/2004
  - Wallace Gilroy Endowed Chair in Nursing 01/2003-05/2004
    - Associate Dean, Undergraduate Program   01/2003-08/2004
- Associate Dean, Student Affairs   06/2003-08/2004
- Assistant Dean, Student Affairs   01/2003-06/2003
- Assistant Professor of Clinical Nursing   06/1983-07/2004

- Director, Basic Track, Undergraduate   01/1988-05/1990
- Director, Learning Resource Center   06/1986-08/1989
- Level Coordinator   08/1982-05/1985
- Instructor   08/1980-06/1983
- Variety/Miami Children's Hospital   06/1978-08/1982
  - Staff Nurse/Charge Nurse

FUNDED RESEARCH

- Sigma Theta Tau International   04/2006
  - Student Centered NCLEX-RN® Preparation: A Program to Enhance Student Success
  - Research Grant, $5000, Principal Investigator
- HRSA, Scholarships for Disadvantaged Students   07/2003
  - University of Miami School of Nursing, $186,000, Principal Investigator
- HRSA, Advanced Educational Nurse Traineeship   07/2003
  - University of Miami School of Nursing, $34,000, Principal Investigator
- Florida Nursing Foundation   07/2002
  - Factors Impacting Role Socialization of New RN Graduates, $750, Principal Investigator

HONORS AND AWARDS (SELECT)

- Florida Nurses Association ICON Award   09/2019
  - Mentor/Role Model ICON
- American Association Colleges of Nursing   2004
  - Helene Fuld Fellow
- Florida Nurses Association   2002
  - Nurse Educator of the Year

- University of Miami   2000
  - Provost's Excellence in Teaching Award
  - First School of Nursing Faculty to Receive
- University of Miami, School of Nursing   1994-2002
  - Numerous Teaching Awards (Students)

PROFESSIONAL ORGANIZATIONS AND POSITIONS (SELECT)

- American Nurses Association   2000-Current
- American Association of Colleges of Nursing   2004-2010
- Florida Nurses Association   2000-Current
  - Chair, Research Special Interest Group   2014-Current
  - Member, Reference Committee   2016-2017
- National Student Nurses Association   2011-Current
- National League of Nursing   2004-2010
- Sigma Theta Tau International,   2012-Current
  Alpha Epsilon Chapter
- Sigma Theta Tau International, Beta Tau Chapter   1980-2012
  - President   2000-2004

PROFESSIONAL AND COMMITTEE SERVICE (LAST 10 YEARS)

- International Committees
  - Sigma Theta Tau International
  - Mentorship Task Force, Lead   2017-Current
  - Content Expert, Sigma Academies   2017-Current
  - Career Center, Lead Advisor   2012-Current
  - Virtual Mentor Cohort Program   Jan-July 2020

- Virtual Mini-Academy: Career Tools — Feb-March 2020
- Virtual Academy, Writing for Publication — April-Aug 2020
- Abstract Reviewer, Biennial; Congress — 2018-2019;
- 2005-2009
- Research/Grants Committee, Ex Officio — 2005-2009
- National Committees
  - Association for Radiologic & Imaging Nursing
  - Editorial Board, *Journal of Radiology Nursing* 2016-Current
- Elsevier Publishing, Nursing — 2016-2019
  - Member, Nursing Advisory Board
- State Committees
  - Florida Nurses Association
  - Research Special Interest Group, Chair — 2014-Current
  - Reference Committee — 2014-2015

PROFESSIONAL SERVICE

- National Student Nurses Association
  - Career Center, In Person/Virtual Conventions 2011-Current
    - Twice/year (250-300 attendees/annual convention; 100 attendees/midyear)
    - Coordinator; Lead Advisor (Volunteer)
- Sigma Theta Tau International
  - Career Center, In Person/Virtual Conferences 2012-Current
    - Twice/year (65 attendees/Biennial Convention; 35 attendees/Research Congress; 30 attendees/Leadership/ Creating Healthy Work Environments)
  - Lead Advisor (Volunteer)
    - Career Advice Virtual/The Circle (2-5 postings per week)

- Free NCLEX Webinars via Sigma Theta Tau International 05/2020-Current
  - Monthly (Average 200 attendees/10 countries/month)
- @NCLEXprof (Lois Marshall) Twitter/Facebook   2009-Current
  - Providing NCLEX Word/Strategies of Day (No Cost)
  - Work with individuals asking for assistance (No Cost)
  - # Followers Twitter 1700; Facebook 1400

REFEREED PUBLICATIONS (LAST 10 YEARS)

- **Marshall, L. S.** (2020; 2019; 2018; 2017; 2016). Quarterly Column, as Editor for Research Column, *Journal of Radiology Nursing.*
  - Priority topics related to Advancing Research and Evidence Based Skills, Abstract Development, Small Grant Funding, and Dissemination as "Tools" Towards Career Advancement
- **Marshall, L. S.** (2016). Broken heart syndrome. *Journal of Radiology Nursing.* 35(2), June 2016, 133-137. https://doi.org/10.1016/j.jradnu.2016.04.002

NON-REFEREED PUBLICATIONS (LAST 10 YEARS)

- **Marshall, L. S.** (2019). "Sigma's career center: Starting point for the rest of your journey," *Reflections on Nursing Leadership.* https://www.reflectionsonnursingleadership.org/features/more-features/sigma-s-career-center-starting-point-for-rest-of-your-journey
- **Marshall, L. S.** (2016). "White Paper: Evidence-Based Nursing Practice," Elsevier Publishing, Clinical Nursing Key, June 2016.

BOOK PUBLICATIONS (LAST 10 YEARS)

- **Marshall, L. S.** *Take Charge of Your Nursing Career.* IN: Sigma Theta Tau International, In Print for Publication, 2021.
- **Marshall, L. S.** (2010). *Take Charge of Your Nursing Career: Open the Door to Your Dreams.* IN: Sigma Theta Tau International, 2010.

REFEREED PRESENTATIONS, INTERNATIONAL (LAST 10 YEARS)

- **Marshall, L. S.** (2021). "Mentorship for Career Advancement," Peer Reviewed Oral Presentation, Sigma Theta Tau International 46th Biennial Convention, Indianapolis, IN, November 6-11, 2021.
- **Marshall, L. S.** (2018). "It's All About the Evidence: Practical Information for Evidence-Based Practice Consumers and Generators," Peer Reviewed Concurrent Paper Presentation, Sigma Theta Tau International 29th International Research Congress, Melbourne, Australia, July 19-23, 2018.
- Howard, M. S., **Marshall, L. S.**, Alexandre, M., Bartlett, R., Bond, M. L., Davidson, P. M., Eviza, K. F., … Slater, L. Z. (2017). "Mentoring and coaching in nursing: How can you make a difference in the profession?" Peer-Reviewed Concurrent Paper Presentation, Sigma Theta Tau International 44th Biennial Convention, Indianapolis, IN, October 29, 2017.
- **Marshall, L. S.** (2016). "Evidence-Based Nursing for Nurse Consumers and Nurse Generators," Peer Reviewed Oral Presentation, Association of Radiology and Interventional Nurses Annual Convention, Vancouver, British Columbia, Canada, April 5, 2016.

REFEREED PRESENTATIONS, NATIONAL (LAST 10 YEARS)

- Howard, M. S., & **Marshall, L. S.** (2018). "Making a mentoring match: Advancing the profession through technology," Peer-Reviewed Poster Presentation, American Nurses Association 2018 Conference, Orlando, FL, March 21-23, 2018.

REFEREED PRESENTATIONS, STATE (LAST 10 YEARS)

- **Marshall, L. S.** (2013). "Research Abstracts, Proposals and Grant Writing," Peer-Reviewed Podium Presentation, Florida Nurses Association, Membership Assembly, Orlando, FL, September 19, 2013.

INVITED PRESENTATIONS, INTERNATIONAL (LAST 10 YEARS)

- **Marshall, L. S.,** (Lead), Lillis, K., Maykut, C. (2021). "Virtual Mini-Academy: Tools for Career Advancement," Sigma Theta Tau International Virtual Academy, Monthly, February-April 2021. (22)
- **Marshall, L. S.** (Lead), Bartle, R., Bond, M., Morin, K. (2021). "Virtual Mentor Cohort Program," Sigma Theta Tau International Virtual Academy, Monthly, January-June 2021. (130).
- **Marshall, L. S.** (2020). "Finding Your Voice Through Scholarly Dissemination," Sigma Theta Tau International, Leadership Academy, Virtual, December 7; 9, 2020.
- **Marshall, L. S.,** Howard, M. (2020). "Career Mentoring and Your Trajectory," Nightingale Challenge, Sigma Theta Tau International, Virtual, October 2020.
- **Marshall, L. S.** (2020). "Virtual Academy: Writing for Publication," Sigma Theta Tau International Virtual Academy, Pilot, Monthly, May- September 2020. (09).

- **Marshall, L. S.,** & Maykut, C. (2020). "Transitioning into Practice: Myths vs Reality," Sigma Theta Tau International, Webinar, June 2020. (74)

- **Marshall, L. S.** (2020). "Mentorship as a Tool for Career Advancement," Sigma Theta Tau International Virtual Mentor Cohort, April 2020. (10)

- **Marshall, L. S.** (2020). "Roles of Mentors and Mentees," Sigma Theta Tau International Virtual Mentor Cohort, February 2020. (10)

- **Marshall, L. S.,** (Lead), Bartle, R., Bond, M., Morin, K. (2020). "Pilot Mentor Cohort Program," Sigma Theta Tau International Virtual Academy, Monthly, January-April 2020. (10 participants). (10)

- **Marshall, L. S.** (2019). "Finding Your Voice Through Scholarly Dissemination," Preconference, 45th Sigma Theta Tau International Biennial Convention, Washington DC, November 2019.

- **Marshall, L. S.** (2019). "Student Engagement," Special Session Presentation, 45th Sigma Theta Tau International Biennial Convention, Washington, DC, November 2019. (50)

- **Marshall, L. S.,** & Marshall, L. S. (2019). "Grants and Mentorship: How One Affects the Other," Special Session Concurrent Paper Presentation, 30th Sigma Theta Tau International Nursing Research Congress, Calgary, Alberta, Canada, July 25-29, 2019. (39)

- **Marshall, L. S.,** Gennaro, S., Melnyk, B. (2019). "Scholarly Writing for Publication," Preconference, 30th International Nursing Research Congress, Calgary, Alberta, Canada, July 25-29, 2019.

- **Marshall, L. S.,** & Howard, M. S. (2019). "Grants and Mentorship: A Mutually Beneficial Partnership," Special Session Concurrent Paper Presentation, Creating Healthy Work Environments 2019 Sigma Theta Tau International Conference, New Orleans, LA, February 22-24, 2019. (40)

- Marshall, L. S., & Howard, M. S. (2018). "Grants and Mentorship: A Mutually Beneficial Partnership," Special Session Concurrent Paper Presentation, Leadership Connection 2018 conference, Indianapolis, IN, September 15-18, 2018. (38)

- Marshall, L. S., & Howard, M. S. (2018). "Grants and Mentorship: A Mutually Beneficial Partnership," Special Session Concurrent Paper Presentation, 29th Sigma Theta Tau International Nursing Research Congress, Melbourne, Australia, July 19-23, 2018. (40)

- Marshall, L. S., Hall, N., Lai, C. K. Y., Howard, M. S. (2018). "Mentoring Experiences," Special Session Concurrent Paper Presentation, 29th Sigma Theta Tau International Nursing Research Congress, Melbourne, Australia, July 19-23, 2018.

- Marshall, L. S. (2017). "Student Engagement," Special Session Presentation, 44th Sigma Theta Tau International Biennial Convention, Indianapolis, IN, November 2017. (50)

- Marshall, L. S. (2017). "Research Abstracts, Proposals, and Grant Writing: Basics from Start to Finish," Special Session, 27th Sigma Theta Tau International Nursing Research Congress, Dublin, Ireland, July 2017. (40)

- Marshall, L. S. (2017). "Managing Your Own Career Potential," Creating Healthy Work Environments 2017 Sigma Theta Tau International Conference, Indianapolis, IN, February 2017.

- Marshall, L. S. (2017). "The Art and Science of Marketing Yourself,"Creating Health Work Environments 2017 Sigma Theta Tau International Conference, Indianapolis, IN, February 2017.

- Marshall, L. S. (2015). "Research Abstracts, Proposals, and Grant Writing: Basics from Start to Finish," Special Session, 43rd Sigma Theta Tau International Biennial Convention, Indianapolis, IN, November 2015.

- Marshall, L. S. (2015). "Student Engagement," Special Session Presentation, 43rd Sigma Theta Tau International Biennial Convention, Indianapolis, IN, November 2015.

- **Marshall, L. S.** (2015). "Research Abstracts, Proposals, and Grant Writing: Basics from Start to Finish," Special Session, 26th Sigma Theta Tau International Nursing Research Congress, San Juan, Puerto Rico, July 2015.
- **Marshall, L. S.** (2013). "Research Abstracts, Proposals, and Grant Writing: Basics from Start to Finish," Special Session, 42nd Sigma Theta Tau International Biennial Convention, 2013, Orlando, FL, November 2013.

INVITED PRESENTATIONS, NATIONAL (LAST 10 YEARS)

- **Marshall, L. S.,** & Howard, M. S. (2020). "Brewing Your Portfolio," Association for Nursing Professional Development, Career Based Web Series, Virtual, October 21, 2020.
- **Marshall, L. S.** (2020). "Faculty-Student Mentorship: Preparation of the Next Generation of Nurses for the Real World," National Student Nurses Association Midyear Convention, Virtual, October 2020. (50)
- **Marshall, L. S.** (2020). "The Art and Science of Marketing Yourself," National Student Nurses Association Midyear Convention, Virtual, October 2020. (74)
- **Marshall, L. S.** (2020). "Navigating the Steps in Advancing Your Education," National Student Nurses Association Midyear Convention, Virtual, October 2020. (44)
- **Marshall, L. S.** (2020). "Faculty-Student Mentorship: Preparation of the Next Generation of Nurses for the Real World," National Student Nurses Association Midyear Convention, Virtual, April 2020. (40)
- **Marshall, L. S.** (2020). "The Art and Science of Marketing Yourself," National Student Nurses Association Annual Convention, Virtual, April 2020. (66)

- Marshall, L. S. (2019). "Faculty-Student Mentorship: Preparation of Next Generation of Novice Nurses and Beyond," National Student Nurses Association Midyear Convention, Chicago, IL, November 2019. (40)

- Marshall, L. S. (2019). "Career Development for New Graduates," Panelist, National Student Nurses Association Midyear Convention, Chicago, IL, November 2019. (82)

- Marshall, L. S. (2019). "The Art and Science of Marketing Yourself," National Student Nurses Association Midyear Convention, Chicago, IL, November 2019. (62)

- Marshall, L. S. (2019). "Advancing Your Nursing Education: ReachingYour Goals Through Higher Education," National Student Nurses Midyear Convention, Chicago, IL, November 2019. (50)

- Marshall, L. S. (2019). "Small Grants: The Keys to Your Research andFunding Trajectories," American Nurses Credentialing Center, MAGNETConference, Funding Panelist, (Representing Sigma Theta Tau International), Orlando, FL, October 2019. (52)

- Marshall, L. S. (2019). "Faculty-Student Mentorship: Preparation of the Next Generation of Nurses for the Real World," National Student Nurses Association Annual Convention, Salt Lake City, UT, April 2019. (55)

- Marshall, L. S. (2019). "The Art and Science of Marketing Yourself," National Student Nurses Association Annual Convention, Salt Lake City, UT, April 2019. (65)

- Marshall, L. S. (2019). "Navigating the Steps in Advancing Your Education," National Student Nurses Association Annual Convention, Salt Lake City, UT, April 2019. (41)

- Marshall, L. S. (2019). "Career Development for New Graduates," Panelist, National Student Nurses Association Annual Convention, Salt Lake City, UT, April 2019. (57)

- Marshall, L. S. (2018). "Faculty-Student Mentorship: Preparation of Next Generation of Novice Nurses and Beyond," National Student Nurses Association Midyear Convention, Louisville, KY, November 2018. (39)

- **Marshall, L. S.** (2018). "Career Development for New Graduates," Panelist, National Student Nurses Association Midyear Convention, Louisville, KY, November 2018. (43)
- **Marshall, L. S.** (2018). "Academic Advancement of Your Career," National Student Nurses Association Midyear Convention, Louisville, KY, November 2018. (31)
- **Marshall, L. S.** (2018). "Advancing Your Nursing Education Goals Through Higher Education," National Student Nurses Association Midyear Convention, Louisville, KY, November 2018. (30)
- **Marshall, L. S.** (2018). "Faculty-Student Mentorship: Preparation of the Next Generation of Nurses for the Real World," National Student Nurses Association Annual Convention, Nashville, TN, April 2018 (60)
- **Marshall, L. S.** (2018). "The Art and Science of Marketing Yourself," National Student Nurses Association Annual Convention, Nashville, TN, April 2018. (84)
- **Marshall, L. S.** (2017). "Faculty-Student Mentorship: Preparation of the Next Generation of Nurses for the Real World," National Student Nurses Association Midyear Convention, San Diego, CA, November 2017. (30)
- **Marshall, L. S.** (2017). "Unique Test Taking Strategies for NCLEX- RN," National Student Nurses Association Midyear Convention, San Diego, CA, November 2017.
- **Marshall, L. S.** (2017). "ADN and Diploma Career Advancement," National Student Nurses Association Midyear Convention, San Diego, CA, November 2017.
- **Marshall, L. S.** (2017). "How to Develop an Evidence-Based Research Project," Webinar, Elsevier Publishing, Clinical Nursing Key, May 2017.
- **Marshall, L. S.** (2017). "Maximizing Your Career Options for FacultyAcademicians," National Student Nurses Association Annual Convention, Dallas, TX, April 2017.

- Marshall, L. S. (2017). "Faculty-Student Mentorship: Preparation of the Next Generation of Nurses for the Real World," National Student Nurses Association Annual Convention, Dallas, TX, April 2017. (60)
- Marshall, L. S. (2017). "Unique Test Taking Strategies for NCLEX- RN," National Student Nurses Association Annual Convention, Dallas, TX, April 2017.
- Marshall, L. S. (2017). "The Art and Science of Marketing Yourself," National Student Nurses Association Annual Convention, Dallas, TX, April 2017.
- Marshall, L. S. (2016). "Faculty-Student Mentorship: Preparation of the Next Generation of Nurses for the Real World," National Student Nurses Association Midyear Convention, Kansas City, MO, November 2016.
- Marshall, L. S. (2016). "Advancing Your Career and Education: A to Z," National Student Nurses Association Midyear Convention, Kansas City, MO, November 2016.
- Marshall, L. S. (2016). "ADN and Diploma Career Advancement," National Student Nurses Association Midyear Convention, Kansas City, MO, November 2016.
- Marshall, L. S. (2016). "How to Develop an Evidence-Based Research Project," Webinar, Elsevier Publishing, Clinical Nursing Key, June 2016. (144)
- Marshall, L. S. (2016). "Creating a Culture of Evidence-Based Practice in Radiology-Imaging Setting," Webinar, Association of Radiology and Imaging Nurses, June 2016. (251)
- Marshall, L. S. (2016). "It's All About the Evidence: Practical Information for Evidence-Based Practice Consumers and Generators," Webinar, Association of Radiology and Imaging Nurses, June 2016. (200)
- Marshall, L. S. (2016). "Faculty-Student Mentorship: Preparation of the Next Generation of Nurses for the Real World," National Student Nurses Association Annual Convention, Orlando, FL, March 2016.

- **Marshall, L. S.** (2016). "Maximizing Your Career Options for Faculty Academicians," National Student Nurses Association Annual Convention, Orlando, FL, March 2016.
- **Marshall, L. S.** (2016). "Advancing Your Career and Education: A to Z," National Student Nurses Association Annual Convention, Orlando, FL, March 2016.
- **Marshall, L. S.** (2016). "Your First Job and Graduate Education," National Student Nurses Association Annual Convention, Orlando, FL, March 2016.
- **Marshall, L. S.** (2015). "Faculty-Student Mentorship: Preparation of the Next Generation of Nurses for the Real World," National Student Nurses Association Midyear Convention, Atlanta, GA, November 2015.
- **Marshall, L. S.** (2015). "Advancing Your Nursing Education: Reaching Your Goals Through Higher Education," National Student Nurses Midyear Convention, Atlanta, GA, November 2015.
- **Marshall, L. S.** (2015). "The Art and Science of Marketing Yourself," National Student Nurses Association Midyear Convention, Atlanta, GA, November 2015.
- **Marshall, L. S.** (2015). "Webinar Series, Evidence-Based Nursing Practice in Home Health." Elsevier Publishing, Clinical Nursing Key, July 2015. (93)
- **Marshall, L. S.** (2015). "Your First Job and Graduate Education," National Student Nurses Association Annual Convention, Phoenix, AZ, April 2015.
- **Marshall, L. S.** (2015). "Faculty-Student Mentorship: Preparation of Next Generation of Novice Nurses and Beyond," National Student Nurses Association Annual Convention, Phoenix, AZ, April 2015 (50)
- **Marshall, L. S.** (2015). "Grant Writing for Faculty," National Student Nurses Association Annual Convention, Phoenix, AZ, April 2015. (50)

- Marshall, L. S. (2014). "Student Evaluation in Nursing Education," National Student Nurses Association Midyear Convention, Portland, OR, November 2014.

- Marshall, L. S. (2014). "Faculty-Student Mentorship: Preparation of Next Generation of Novice Nurses and Beyond," National Student Nurses Association Midyear Convention, Portland, OR, November 2014. (32)

- Marshall, L. S. (2014). "The Art and Science of Marketing Yourself," National Student Nurses Association Midyear Convention, Portland, OR, November 2014.

- Marshall, L. S. (2013-2014). "Webinar Series, Evidence-Based Nursing Practice, Creating an Evidence-Based Culture, Developing an Evidence-Based Research Project, Critical Analysis and Evaluation of Evidence-Based Research." Elsevier Publishing, Clinical Nursing Key. May; November 2013-2014. (115)

- Marshall, L. S. (2013). "Student Evaluation in Nursing Education," National Student Nurses Association Midyear Convention, Louisville, KY, November 2013.

- Marshall, L. S. (2013). "Faculty-Student Mentorship: Preparation of the Next Generation of Nurses for the Real World," National Student Nurses Association Midyear Convention, Louisville, KY, November 2013.

- Marshall, L. S. (2013). "The Art and Science of Marketing Yourself," National Student Nurses Association Midyear Convention, Louisville, KY, November 2013.

- Marshall, L. S. (2013). "Your First Job and Graduate Education," National Student Nurses Association Midyear Convention, Louisville, KY, November 2013.

- Marshall, L. S. (2013). "Advancing Your Career and Education: A to Z," National Student Nurses Association Annual Convention, Charlotte, NC, April 2013.

- Marshall, L. S. (2013). "Faculty-Student Mentorship: Preparation of New Graduates for the Nursing Marketplace," Charlotte, NC, April 2013.

- **Marshall, L. S.** (2013). "The Art and Science of Marketing Yourself," National Student Nurses Association Annual Convention, Charlotte, NC, April 2013.
- **Marshall, L. S.** (2012). "Faculty-Student Mentorship: Preparation of the Next Generation of Nurses for the Real World," National Student Nurses Association Midyear Convention, San Diego, CA, November 2012.
- **Marshall, L. S.** (2012). "Student Evaluation in Nursing Education," National Student Nurses Association Midyear Convention, San Diego, CA, November 2012.
- **Marshall, L. S.** (2012). "ADN and Diploma Career Advancement," National Student Nurses Association Midyear Convention, San Diego, CA, November 2012.
- **Marshall, L. S.** (2012). "Advancing Your Career and Education: A to Z," National Student Nurses Association Midyear Convention, San Diego, CA, November 2012.
- **Marshall, L. S.** (2012). "Mapping Out Your Career: Endless Possibilities," National Geriatric Nursing Association Annual Convention, Baltimore, MD, October 2012. (64)
- **Marshall, L. S.** (2012). "Faculty-Student Mentorship," National Student Nurses Association Annual Convention, Pittsburg, PA, April 2012.
- **Marshall, L. S.** (2012). "Advancing Your Career and Education: A to Z," National Student Nurses Association Annual Convention, Pittsburgh, PA, April 2012.
- **Marshall, L. S.** (2012). "The Art and Science of Marketing Yourself," National Student Nurses Association Annual Convention, Pittsburg, PA, April 2012.

INVITED PRESENTATIONS, STATE/LOCAL (LAST 10 YEARS)

- Marshall, L. S. (2021). "The Art and Science of Marketing Yourself," Virtual, Lehigh Carbon Community College, Schnecksville, PA, January 15, 2021. (96)

- Marshall, L. S. (2020). "Finding Your Professional Self and Voice in Your Career," Graduation, Keynote Address, San Francisco State University School of Nursing, Virtual, December 5, 2020.

- Marshall, L. S. (2020). "Finding Your Professional Self and Voice in Your Career," Induction Keynote Address, Sigma Theta Tau International Chapter, San Francisco State University School of Nursing, Virtual, May 2020.

- Marshall, L. S. (2020). "Writing Abstracts: Process for Success," Florida Nurses Association, Webinar, April and May 2020. (46/32)

- Marshall, L. S. (2019). "Professional Career Development: Endless Possibilities," University of Miami School of Nursing, RN-BSN Leadership Class, Coral Gables, FL, October 21, 2019. (30)

- Marshall, L. S. (2019). "Writing Abstracts: Process for Success," Florida Nurses Association, Webinar, April, and May 2019. (34/30)

- Marshall, L. S. (2018). "Writing Abstracts: Process for Success," Florida Nurses Association, Webinar, April, and May 2018. (29/19)

- Marshall, L. S. (2017). "Writing Abstracts: Process for Success," Florida Nurses Association, Webinar, April, and May 2017. (25/18)

- Marshall, L. S. (2017). "Faculty Development Workshop: Test Design and Construction Towards NCLEX and Beyond," Arizona College, Mesa, AZ, January 2017. (15)

- Marshall, L. S. (2016). "Writing Abstracts: Process for Success," The Ohio State University College of Nursing, Webinar, July 2016. (28)

- **Marshall, L. S.** (2016). "Writing Abstracts: Process for Success," Florida Nurses Association, Webinar, April and May 2016. (20/17)
- **Marshall, L. S.** (2016). ""Faculty Development Workshop: Developing a Concept-Based Curriculum," Oakland Community College, Detroit, MI, January 2016.
- **Marshall, L. S.** (2016). "The Art and Science of Marketing Yourself," Georgia Association of Nursing Students, Atlanta, GA, January 2016. (42)
- **Marshall, L. S.** (2016). "Unique Test Taking Strategies for the NCLEX-RN," Georgia Association of Nursing Students, Atlanta, GA, January 2016. (42)
- **Marshall, L. S.** (2015). "It's All About the Evidence: Practical Information for Evidence-Based Practice Consumers and Generators," Florida Nurses Association, Research and Evidence-Based Nursing Annual Conference, Orlando, FL, July 2015. (25)
- **Marshall, L. S.** (2014). "The Art and Science of Marketing Yourself," Sigma Theta Tau International University of Portland Chapter, Portland, OR, November 2014.
- **Marshall, L. S.** (2014). "Unique Test Taking Strategies for NCLEX- RN," Arkansas State Nursing Students Association Annual Convention, Little Rock, AR, October 2014.
- **Marshall, L. S.** (2014). "The Art and Science of Marketing Yourself," Arkansas State Nursing Students Association Annual Convention, Little Rock, AR, October 2014.
- **Marshall, L. S.** (2014). "Pediatric and Family Care Nursing," Arkansas State Nursing Students Association Annual Convention, Little Rock, AR, October 2014.
- **Marshall, L. S.** (2014). "The Art and Science of Marketing Yourself," University of Illinois School of Nursing, Rockford, IL, June 2014.
- **Marshall, L. S.** (2014). "The Art and Science of Marketing Yourself," Sigma Theta Tau International University of Portland Chapter, Portland, OR, February 2014.

- Marshall, L. S. (2014). "Research Abstracts, Proposals and Grant Writing: Basics from Start to Finish," University of North Florida, Sigma Research Day, Jacksonville, FL, February 2014.
- Marshall, L. S. (2014). "The Art and Science of Marketing Yourself," Virginia Nursing Students Association Annual Convention, Richmond, VA, January 2014.
- Marshall, L. S. (2014). "Pediatric and Family Care Nursing," Virginia Nursing Students Association Annual Convention, Richmond, VA, January 2014.
- Marshall, L. S. (2013). "All of the Pieces of You: Integrated to Fit," Keynote Address, Arkansas State Nursing Students Association Annual Convention, Little Rock, AR, October 2013. (106)
- Marshall, L. S. (2013). "Pediatric and Family Care Nursing," Arkansas State Nursing Students Association Annual Convention, Little Rock, AR, October 2013.
- Marshall, L. S. (2013). "Pediatric Neurology: The Practice of Nursing," Arkansas State Nursing Students Association Annual Convention, Little Rock, AR, October 2013.
- Marshall, L. S. (2013). "Beginning a Professional Career," Florida Student Nurses Association Annual Convention, Plenary Speaker, Daytona Beach, FL, October 2013. (80)
- Marshall, L. S. (2013). "The Art and Science of Marketing Yourself," Florida Student Nurses Association Annual Convention, Daytona Beach, FL, October 2013.
- Marshall, L. S. (2013). "Faculty Development Workshop: Test Design and Construction Towards NCLEX and Beyond," City Colleges of Chicago, Chicago, IL, February 2013. (22)
- Marshall, L. S. (2012). "Nursing Outside of the Box," Maryland Association of Nursing Students Annual Convention, Baltimore, MD, January 26, 2012.

EXAMPLE OF BLANK CV

EXAMPLE OF BLANK CV

CURRICULUM VITAE
YOUR NAME, DEGREES/CREDENTIALS
DATE OF CV

EDUCATION

LICENSURE AND CERTIFICATION

PROFESSIONAL EXPERIENCE

FUNDED RESEARCH

HONORS AND AWARDS

PROFESSIONAL ORGANIZATIONS AND POSITIONS

PROFESSIONAL AND COMMITTEE SERVICE

    INTERNATIONAL

    NATIONAL

    STATE

PROFESSIONAL SERVICE

REFEREED PUBLICATIONS

NON-REFEREED PUBLICATIONS

BOOK PUBLICATIONS

REFEREED PRESENTATIONS, INTERNATIONAL

REFEREED PRESENTATIONS, NATIONAL

REFEREED PRESENTATIONS, STATE

INVITED PRESENTATIONS, INTERNATIONAL

INVITED PRESENTATIONS, NATIONAL

INVITED PRESENTATIONS, STATE

D

SAMPLE COVER LETTERS

Jackie M. Hammocks, BSN, RN
3421 SW 49 Terrace
Coral Gables, FL 33143

May 23, 2021

Philip Costello, MSN, RN
Nurse Recruiter
Boston Children's Hospital
300 Longwood Avenue
Boston, MA 02115

Dear Mr. Costello,

Please accept the attached resumé as part of the application for one of the new graduate nurse positions that were advertised at your booth at the Career Expo, National Student Nurses' Association Convention, April 2021. I recently graduated from the University of Miami School of Nursing baccalaureate program with honors. In addition to my 15-week practicum experience on a pediatric medical-surgical unit, I worked for one year as a nurse extern at a children's hospital in Miami, FL. I was lucky enough to have exceptional registered nurse mentors who have prepared me clinically and professionally for my first position as a registered nurse following my graduation and licensure.

My desire to work in pediatrics developed when I experienced nursing care as a patient myself when I was in my early teens. While most of my experiences were positive, some experiences spurred me to think, "I know I can do better." I didn't like being seen as my "health alteration" and not a person. From that very moment on, I knew I wanted to care for pediatric clients with respect and an acknowledgment that no matter their healthcare situation, they were children or adolescents with a unique set of needs and a personality of their own that needed to be considered with every interaction. I have taken that approach in all my clinical experiences as a student and will continue to take that approach in my nursing career.

I would appreciate an opportunity to interview for one of the available positions in the new graduate program at your institution. I understand that Boston Children's Hospital has one of the best new graduate nursing programs in the state, providing a 16-week orientation program with a preceptor. I have spoken to several past participants in the program who have said that your orientation eased their role socialization and allowed them to refine their new skills, in the broadest sense, and experiences prior to taking on the responsibilities of an independent registered nurse.

I look forward to hearing back from you at your earliest convenience to set up an interview with you and your staff. I am now living in the Boston area, so I can meet in person at whatever time works best for you. If you have any questions prior to that time, please do not hesitate to contact me.

Sincerely,
Jackie M. Hammocks, BSN, RN

Lauren Janofsky, PhD, RN, ANEF
13465 SW 112 Avenue
Miami, FL 33186

May 15, 2021

Jane Alexander, PhD, RN, FAAN
Associate Dean
Central Florida University
School of Nursing
1500 Sycamore Drive
Orlando, FL 32801

Dear Dr. Alexander,

Please accept the attached curriculum vitae as part of the application for one of the full-time research faculty positions advertised in the most recent edition of the *Journal of Nursing Scholarship*. I believe that I am well qualified for this position. I have had several research positions in my career, working on federally funded grants through my positions in both private and public clinical and academic institutions. I have been responsible for data collection, data analysis, and development of research reports, and I have collaborated on more than 10 publications related to such research. I completed my PhD from Emory University School of Nursing in 2019, which strengthened my research skills and focus. In addition, I was able to develop the skills necessary to work effectively as a nurse educator through the successful completion of higher education cognate coursework during my PhD program.

I would appreciate an opportunity to interview for one of the available full-time research faculty positions. Central Florida University has distinguished itself as a leader in nursing education and collaborative research. Central Florida University is just the place where I see myself contributing and growing as a nursing academician.

I look forward to hearing from you at your earliest convenience to set up an appointment for an interview with you and your faculty. If you have any questions prior to that time, please do not hesitate to contact me.

Sincerely,
Lauren Janofsky, PhD, RN, ANEF

PERSONAL PHILOSOPHY EXAMPLE: PHILOSOPHY OF TEACHING

"Teach as you wish to be taught [nurse as you wish to be nursed]. Remember that with each interaction, with each student [patient] experience, in that moment in time, you the educator [nurse], give them a piece of yourself, your knowledge and skill, your caring and compassion, something no one else can give and that might not be shared without your presence."

–Lois S. Marshall, 1980

Teaching, like nursing, is both an art and a science. Teaching requires a comprehensive approach to engaging students in the learning process. Teaching requires mutual respect, an imparting of expertise in a particular area(s), teacher and learner accountability, flexibility, a capacity to listen, not just hear, and the willingness to extend oneself beyond the obvious and stimulate the learner to independently think and practice the art and science of nursing.

I am honored to have the opportunity each day to participate in the profession of nursing education in a university environment. Since I began my teaching career in 1980, I have seen my role as an educator become more multifaceted, constantly growing and changing, and continually exciting and challenging. Each and every day that I teach an individual student or groups of students in the classroom and/or clinical setting, I find that I am more excited than the day before. A glimmer in the eye of a student who has answered a question correctly about a disease process, a smile from a student and a patient when the "nurse-patient" connection has been made for the first time, or a comment from a nursing colleague in practice about a student who has made a difference on a nursing staff or a patient/family are some of the reasons that I educate nursing students and why it is the most satisfying and rewarding role for me.

I find the teaching of nursing students from all walks of life, with their diversity, uniqueness, and excitement for learning, is what drives my teaching career. The teaching-learning process requires a collaborative effort on the part of both the teacher and the student. There must be mutual respect between the teacher and the learner. The teacher and learner must always listen—listen to assess, listen to counsel, listen to teach effectively and efficiently. The teacher must be flexible in both teaching style and the methods of working with individual students to bring out their strengths and strengthen their weaknesses. The teacher must be willing to teach.

I believe that my strengths in teaching include my enthusiasm for teaching and my enjoyment of the teaching-learning process; my use of a variety of teaching strategies to address the needs of individual students and groups of students; my willingness to listen and assist students throughout the teaching-learning process in nursing school, not just in the classroom, but as they move through the program; and my ability to impart my expertise in nursing to students in a manner that is positive, non-judgmental, and always fair. While students in a nursing program are part of a large class of students, they, too, are individuals with their own strengths and weaknesses, and their own learning needs that must be addressed. Students need a teacher, a role model, a facilitator, and a motivator. I truly believe that if you value students as individuals and respect them, they will value themselves, their educational endeavors, and their potential future contributions to their chosen profession.

As an educator in the nursing profession, the teaching-learning process goes beyond the classroom to include the clinical setting. I must be an expert in the teaching of theoretical knowledge with practical examples for practice and must also be the role model and expert in the clinical setting in which the students and I are responsible for the quality of care of patients. Students must be able to see the integral connection between theory and clinical practice. Classes must reflect both the content of the course and the critical thinking skills necessary to think as a nursing professional in a variety of clinical situations. Teaching in a nursing curriculum, at any level, requires a strong theoretical frame-work from which the student can build; the practical application of this content; and the ability to analyze, synthesize, and critically think. I believe that I continue to make this an essential component of each course that I teach, for one component without the other does not pro-vide students with a realistic framework on which to base their future nursing practice. I must cover the most up-to-date materials, from both a research perspective and a clinical perspective, to ensure that students are prepared for the current and future healthcare system.

I use a variety of teaching strategies to stimulate ideas in my students. I draw out their critical-thinking abilities and prepare them to best learn and then use the materials presented to them. Lectures are far from the only method of teaching. Weaving in clinical examples, in-process re-search projects, journal presentations, and case studies allows students to get excited about the material and see the content's worthiness in their chosen profession at a baccalaureate level, a graduate level, and as I begin to prepare the future nurse educator.

In closing, the greatest reward of being a nurse educator for me is to see students grow and mature as learners, as people, and as professionals. When I walk through the many clinical sites that I use, I see graduates—former students of mine who at one time sat in my classroom scared and inhibited, but seeking a nursing education—now making a difference in clinical practice, research, administration, and teaching. As with the caterpillar in the cocoon that is nourished and cared for, the beautiful butterfly emerges—independent and prepared for what the future will bring. I know that if I have somehow contributed to their development into nursing professionals, then I have successfully done my job, and I take great pride in that. My students are the future of nursing and healthcare at all levels, and I am proud to play an integral part in that future.

F

FORMAT FOR DEVELOPING YOUR NURSING CAREER IDENTITY

Here, you can fill in areas that are relatable to your role, scope of work, and/or goals and criteria for evaluation. This will assist you in highlighting what areas you are working on and accomplishments to be discussed.

FIGURE F.1   Here, you can put particular components of the overall role you need to be focusing on.

G

MENTORING AGREEMENT

Mentoring Agreement

This agreement is between the Mentor,_____, and the Mentee,_____. The mentorship partnership will begin on (Date)_____and conclude on (Date)_____.

We will attempt to meet at least_____time(s) per month. If one or both of us cannot attend a scheduled meeting, we agree to notify one another in advance.

By signing this document, I am agreeing to participate in this mentoring partnership voluntarily.

By signing this document, I acknowledge that any sensitive issues we discuss will be confidential.

If one of us determines that terminating our partnership is necessary, we agree to abide by one another's decision.

We mutually agree to work toward accomplishing the following during our mentorship partnership:

Overall Goal:_____

_____

Objectives: (Create list, and be sure to include measurable terms)

_____   _____

Mentor   Mentee

_____   _____

Date   Date

INDEX

NOTE: *Page references with an f are figures; page references with a t are tables.*

A

academic education, 37. *See also* education
academies, finding, 93–95
accountability, social media and, 140
activities, resumés, 16
addresses, including on documents, 6
advancing education, 68–70. *See also* education
    clinical nurse leader (CNL), 76
    clinical nurse specialist (CNS), 75–76
    completing applications for, 84–86
    interviewing programs, 84
    narrowing options, 83
    nurse educators, 74–75
    nurse practitioners, 74
    nursing administrators, 75
    post-doctoral fellowships, 127–128
    process for, 70–86
    program offerings, 82–83
    researching degrees, 80–81
    selecting programs, 86
    studying abroad, 132
    what degree to pursue, 71–80
advertising, 182–184
advice, sharing medical, 137, 138
advocacy
    political, 136, 161–162
    using your voice, 158–160 (*see also* voice)
agreements, mentoring, 113
American Medical Association, 158
American Nurses Association, 81
American Nurses Credentialing Center, 97
American Organization for Nursing Leadership (AONL), 75
applications
    completing for advanced

    education, 84–86
    for continuing professional development, 38f
    development, 172
associate degree in nursing (ASN), 83
automatic tracking systems (ATSs), 5
    curriculum vitae (CV), 6
    resumés, 5
awards
    portfolios, 32, 44–46 (*see also* portfolios)
    resumés, 13, 15–16

B

benefits of social media, 137, 139–141
billing, medical, 170
bios, adding (social media), 149
birth coaching, 171
branding, 136, 137. *See also* social media
    audiences, 144–145
    core values, 142
    future endeavors, 147
    goals, 145–146
    identifying, 141–148
    mission statements, 146–147
    selecting platforms for, 148
    vision statements, 145–146
budgeting, 15
bullet points, formatting, 14
business, starting, 167. *See also* entrepreneurship

C

Canada
    post-doctoral fellowships, 127–128
    relocating to, 125, 126–127
career-building websites, 8
Career Center at Sigma Theta Tau International Honor Society of Nursing, 8, 96, 111, 124
careers
    continuing education, 89, 90

development, 123, 124
education. *See* education
international nurses, 123, 124
job seeking, 3 (*see also* job seeking)
marketing, 2–4 (*see also* marketing)
nursing identity, 63 (*see also* nursing identity)
portfolios, 31, 32 (*see also* portfolios)
resumés (*see* resumés)
risks of social media on, 137–138
social media (*see* social media)
strategies for dissemination, 155–158
work-life balance, 187, 188
Centers for Disease Control and Prevention (CDC), 131
certificate programs, 91
certification, 91
  continuing education, 97–99
  continuing professional development, 97–99
  examinations, 97
  obtaining, 33
  portfolios, 39
  resumés, 10–11
Character Strength Survey, 143, 144
chart coding, 170
child services, 171
clinical nurse leader (CNL), 73, 76
clinical nurse specialist (CNS), 73, 75–76
coaching
  birth, 171
  comparing to mentoring, 105 (*see also* mentoring)
  prenatal, 171
  wellness, 171
Cogan, Robin, 159
collaboration, 44. *See also* mentoring; publications
  mentoring, 112 (*see also* mentoring)
  social media, 136 (*see also* social media)

using your voice, 154–155 (*see also* voice, using your)
Commission on Graduates of Foreign Nursing Students, 127
committee work, portfolios, 49
communication, 15
  career identities, 32 (*see also* portfolios)
  dissemination, 155–158 (*see also* voice, using your)
  procedures (for education programs), 84
community service
  portfolios, 50–51
  resumés, 18
components of portfolios
  awards, 44–46
  certifications, 37–39
  committee work, 49
  community service, 50–51
  continuing professional development, 37–39
  curriculum vitae (CV), 35
  education, 37
  employment history, 39–41
  fellowships, 46
  grants, 48
  honors, 44–46
  licenses, 37–39
  military service, 49–50
  miscellaneous section of, 51–54
  nursing consultation, 52
  personal philosophies, 36
  presentations, 42–44
  professional organizations, 41–42
  publications, 44
  reflective statements, 53–54
  research, 46–48
  resumés, 35
  scholarships, 46
  summary statements, 53–54
components of resumés, 9
  activities, 16
  awards/honors, 13, 15–16
  certification/licensure, 10–11
  community service, 18

curriculum vitae (CV) (*see*
  curriculum vitae [CV])
  education, 12–13
  experience, 13–15
  expertise, 18–19
  goals/objective statements, 9–10
  presentations/publications, 16–18
  Professional Activities, 12
  professional organizations, 16
  references, 19
  special skills, 18–19
  volunteer service, 18
conferences
  attending, 95–97
  finding mentors, 112
  international, 133
connections
  finding mentors, 112
  mentoring, 118
  searching international jobs, 131,
    133
  social media (*see* social media)
constructive criticism, 115
consultation
  nursing, 52
  for school systems, 172
contacts
  finding mentors via, 112
  management, 149
continuing education, 89, 90
  attending conferences, 95–97
  certification, 97–99
  credentials, 97–99
  finding programs, 93–95
  reasons for, 92–93
  types of, 91
continuing professional development,
  37–39, 89, 90. *See also* education
  attending conferences, 95–97
  certification, 97–99
  credentials, 97–99
  finding programs, 93–95
  reasons for, 92–93
  types of, 91
contracts, mentoring, 113
core values, 142, 143*t*, 144

courses. *See also* education
  finding, 93–95
  tracking, 38*f*
cover letters, 21, 226–228
Covey, Stephen, 145
COVID-19, 22, 74, 84, 158
  Pandemic Task Force, 161
  social media and, 138
  virtual conferences and, 96
  working from home, 177
  work-life balance and, 192
credentials, 91
  continuing education, 97–99
  continuing professional
    development, 97–99
  portfolios, 39
crowd surfing, 149
curriculum vitae (CV), 3, 4–8, 85
  automatic tracking systems (ATSs),
    6
  cultural impact on, 125
  editing, 8
  examples of, 202–224
  formatting, 19–21
  portfolios, 32, 35 (*see also*
    portfolios)
  resources, 8
  writing, 7
customer service, 15

D

deadlines, meeting, 181
defining nursing identities, 62–65
degrees, 12. *See also* education
  associate degree in nursing (ASN),
    83
  clinical nurse leader (CNL), 76
  clinical nurse specialist (CNS),
    75–76
  deciding what to pursue, 71–80
  doctor of education (EdD), 73, 77
  doctor of nursing practice (DNP/
    DrNP), 73, 77, 78
  doctor of nursing science (DNS or
    DNSc), 73, 77

doctor of philosophy (PhD), 73, 76, 78
doctor of science in nursing (DSN), 77
nurse educators, 74–75
nurse practitioners, 74
nursing administrators, 75
program offerings, 82–83
researching, 80–81
terminal, 72, 76–80
types of, 73, 80–81
design
  examinations, 172
  healthcare facilities, 173
  web sites, 184
development. *See also* education
  applications, 172
  continuing professional, 37–39
  international nursing careers, 123, 124
  social media (*see* social media)
diets, eating right, 191
dissemination, 155–158
doctor of education (EdD), 73, 77
doctor of nursing practice (DNP), 73, 77, 78
doctor of nursing practice (DrNP), 73
Doctor of Nursing Practice projects, 48
doctor of nursing science (DNS or DNSc), 73, 77
doctor of philosophy (PhD), 73, 76, 78
doctor of science in nursing (DSN), 77
Doctors Without Borders, 133
documents
  certification, 33 (*see also* certification)
  cover letters, 21 (*see also* cover letters)
  cultural impact on, 125
  curriculum vitae (CV), 3, 4–8
  editing, 8
  including addresses, 6
  portfolios (*see* portfolios)
  publications (*see* publications)

resumés, 3, 4–8
submitting, 4, 84–86
tracking, 5

E

editing
  curriculum vitae (CV), 8
  medical, 172, 173
  mission statements, 146–147
  resumés, 8
education
  awards/honors, 13, 15–16
  career portfolios and, 33 (*see also* portfolios)
  clinical nurse leader (CNL), 76
  clinical nurse specialist (CNS), 75–76
  completing applications for, 84–86
  continuing, 89, 90 (*see also* continuing education)
  continuing professional development, 37–39
  deciding to further, 68–70
  gaining expertise, 67, 68
  international options in, 132
  interviewing programs, 84
  narrowing options, 83
  nurse educators, 74–75
  nurse practitioners, 74
  nursing administrators, 75
  portfolios, 37
  post-doctoral fellowships, 127–128
  process for advancing, 70–86
  program offerings, 82–83
  researching degrees, 80–81
  resumés, 12–13
  selecting programs, 86
  sharing resources, 141
  studying abroad, 132
  terminal degrees, 72, 76–80
  what degree to pursue, 71–80
employment
  career portfolios, 32, 33 (*see also* portfolios)
  cover letters, 21

entrepreneurship, 184–186 (*see also* entrepreneurship)
histories (in portfolios), 39–41
interviews, 22–29
marketing, 2–4 (*see also* marketing)
resumés (*see* resumés)
risks of social media on, 137–138
English, speaking, 130
Entrepreneur, 176
entrepreneurship, 167
    advertising, 182–184
    finances, 179–180
    health insurance, 181
    marketing, 182–184
    opportunities for, 170–174
    personnel, 184–186
    planning, 178–179
    resources, 175, 176
    starting, 175–178
    taking on new challenges, 168–169
    workloads, 181–182
evaluations
    future endeavors, 147
    mentoring, 114
    mission statements, 146–147
    performance, 33
evidence-based projects, 48
examinations, 91
    certification, 97
    designing, 172
    National League for Nursing, 98
Excel for continuing professional development, 38*f*
exercise, 191
experience
    mentorship, 109 (*see also* mentoring)
    resumés, 13–15
expertise
    certification programs and, 98
    dissemination, 155–158
    gaining, 67, 68 (*See also* education)
    resumés, 18–19

F
fellowships
    portfolios, 46
    post-doctoral, 127–128
finances, entrepreneurship, 179–180
forensic nursing, 170
formal education, 37. *See also* education
formal presentations, 42. *See also* presentations
formatting
    bullet points, 14
    cover letters, 21
    curriculum vitae (CV), 19–21
    keywords, 5
    resumés, 3, 9
    subsections in resumés, 13

G
gaining expertise, 67, 68. *See also* education
Gallwey, Timothy, 145
Global Health Jobs and Opportunities (CDC), 131
global mentorship, 118–121. *See also* mentoring
goals
    branding, 145–146
    resumés, 9–10
government agency resources, 129
graduate entry, 72
Graduate Record Examination, 84
grants, portfolios, 48
groups, social media, 140, 149. *See also* social media

H
hard skills, 6
headshots, social media, 148–149
healthcare facility design, 173
healthcare policymakers, 79
health insurance, entrepreneurship, 181

help, 8. *See also* resources
histories, employment, 35, 39–41. *See also* portfolios
holistic care, 171
home, working from, 177
honors
    portfolios, 32, 44–46 (*see also* portfolios)
    resumés, 13, 15–16

I

identities. *See* nursing identity
images, social media, 148–149
incorporation, pros and cons of, 180
infodemic, 138
informal presentations, 42. *See also* presentations
The Inner Game of Work (Gallwey), 145
in-person interviews, 22
Institute for Credentialing Excellence, 97
insurance, health, 181
integrative reviews, 48
International Academy of Nursing Editors, 17
international conferences, 133
international nurses, 123, 124
    cultural impact on careers, 125–126
    post-doctoral fellowships, 127–128
    relocating across the globe, 128–132
    relocating to North America, 126–127
    requirements for, 129
interpreting, 173
interviews, 22–29
    concluding, 28–29
    interviewing degree programs, 84
    preparing for, 23–25
    processes, 25–28
introduction, cover letters, 21

J

Japan, licenses in, 131
job seeking
    career portfolios, 32, 33 (*see also* portfolios)
    cover letters, 21
    for international nursing jobs, 131, 132–133
    interviews, 22–29
    marketing, 2–4 (*see also* marketing)
    resumés (*see* resumés)
journaling, 144
journals. *See also* publications
    finding mentors, 120
    predatory, 17

K-L

keywords, 5

languages
    learning, 130
    speaking English, 130
leadership, 15
legal consultation, 170, 174
licenses
    in Japan, 131
    NCLEX-RN, 130
    portfolios, 32, 39 (*see also* portfolios)
    relocating to North America, 127
    resumés, 10–11
    social media policies, 137
LinkedIn, 118, 148. *See also* social media
lists, making, 142

M

management, 15
    branding, 141 (*see also* branding)
    contacts (social media), 149
    education, 68–70 (*see also* education)

international nurses, 123, 124 (*see also* international nurses)
mentorship expectations, 109
nursing administrators, 75
manuscripts, 44. *See also* publications; writing
maps, career, 65. *See also* nursing identity
marketing
 documents, 3, 4–8 (*see also* documents)
 entrepreneurship, 182–184
 reasons for, 2
 where to start, 2–4
master of nursing (MN) degree, 72
master of science in nursing (MSN) degree, 72
media (mainstream), advocacy and, 158–160. *See also* social media
medical billing, 170
medical editing, 172, 173
medical reviews, 170
medical staffing, 170
medical writing, 172, 173
mental health counseling, 171
mentoring, 33, 101, 102–103, 133
 agreement example, 236
 benefits of, 108–110
 characteristics of mentors, 107
 comparing to coaching, 105
 constructive criticism, 115
 definition of, 104–105
 evaluations, 114
 finding, 111–113
 networking, 118
 obstacles, 116–117
 opportunities for, 110
 planning, 113–115
 promoting, 115–116
 resources, 122
 roles and responsibilities of, 105–108
 SMART goals, 114
Mentorship Cohort (Sigma), 110
Mentorship mini-Academy (Sigma), 110

military service, portfolios, 49–50
mind-mapping, 142, 143*f*
miscellaneous section of portfolios, 51–54
mission statements, 146–147
mission trips, 133

N

narratives, 32, 48. *See also* portfolios
National Association for the Self-Employed, 176
National Association of Pediatric Nurse Practitioners, 98
National Council of State Boards of Nursing, 127
National Institute of Nursing Research, 79
National Institutes of Health, 79
National League for Nursing, 98
National Organization of Nurse Practitioner Faculties, 74
NCLEX-RN, 72, 130
networking
 as an investment, 139
 expanding, 150
 finding mentors, 112
 mentoring, 118
 searching international jobs, 131, 133
 social media (*see* social media)
 using your voice, 162–164 (*see also* voice)
North America
 moving to, 125, 126–127
 post-doctoral fellowships, 127–128
numbers, licenses, 10–11
nurse educators, 74–75
Nurse Licensure Compact, 10
nurse practitioners, 74
Nurses Without Borders, 133
nursing
 advocacy for, 160 (*see also* advocacy)
 consultation, 52

continuing professional
    development, 37–39
designing examinations, 172
education, 12–13
entrepreneurship, 167 (*see also*
    entrepreneurship)
format for identities, 234
international nurses, 123, 124 (*see
    also* international nurses)
licenses, 10–11
mentoring, 101, 102–103 (*see also*
    mentoring)
portfolios (*see* portfolios)
resumés (*see* resumés)
searching (for positions), 3 (*see
    also* job seeking)
skills, 15
using your voice (*see* voice, using
    your)
work-life balance, 187, 188
nursing administrators, 75
Nursing and Midwifery Board of
    Australia, 129
Nursing and Midwifery Board of
    Ireland, 129
Nursing and Midwifery Council of the
    United Kingdom, 129
Nursing Council of Hong Kong, 129
Nursing Council of New Zealand,
    129
nursing identity, 60, 61
    defining, 62–65
    format for, 234
    path of nursing journeys, 61–62
    schematics (planning), 63, 64*f*, 65*f*
Nursing Journal Directory, 17

O

objective statements, resumés, 9–10
obstacles to mentoring, 116–117
open-access journals, 17
organizations (professional),
    resumés, 16. *See also* professional
    organizations

P

Pandemic Task Force, COVID-19,
    161
partnerships, mentoring, 101, 102–
    103
peer reviews, journals, 17
performance evaluations, 33
personal philosophies
    example of, 229–232
    in portfolios, 36
personnel, entrepreneurship, 184–186
*Peterson's Complete Guide to
    Colleges,* 81
pictures, social media, 148–149
planning
    entrepreneurship, 178–179
    mentoring, 113–115
    nursing identities, 63, 64*f*, 65*f*
podcasts, contributions to, 42
political advocacy, 136, 161–162
portfolios, 34*f*
    awards, 44–46
    certification, 39
    committee work, 49
    community service, 50–51
    components of, 34–35
    continuing professional
        development, 37–39
    credentials, 39
    cultural impact on, 125
    curriculum vitae (CV), 35
    education, 37
    employment histories, 39–41
    fellowships, 46
    grants, 48
    honors, 44–46
    licenses, 39
    military service, 49–50
    miscellaneous section of, 51–54
    nursing consultation, 52
    personal philosophies, 36
    presentations, 42–44
    process of putting together, 54–55
    professional organizations, 41–42
    publications, 44

reasons for, 32–34
reflective statements, 53–54
research, 46–48
resources, 55
resumés, 35
scholarships, 46
summary statements, 53–54
post-doctoral fellowships, 127–128
Post-it portfolios, 34. *See also*
    portfolios
posts, social media, 150. *See also*
    social media
predatory journals, 17
prenatal coaching, 171
Prescribed Pediatric Extended Care
    (PPEC) facility, 169
presentations
    portfolios, 35, 42–44 (*see also*
        portfolios)
    resumés, 16–18
processes, mentoring, 105–108
Professional Activities (resumés), 12
professional organizations
    finding mentors, 110
    portfolios, 41–42
    resumés, 16
    using your voice, 160 (*see also*
        voice, using your)
profile pictures, social media, 148–
    149
programs, 93–95. *See also* education
projects, 46. *See also* research
promoting mentoring, 115–116
promotion, tenure, and reappointment
    (PTR), 63, 65f
publications
    documenting, 46
    portfolios, 44
    resumés, 16–18

Q

quality improvement
    projects, 48
    reviews, 170
quizzes, 143

R

references, resumés, 19
reflective statements, 53–54
relationships, mentoring, 101, 102–
    103
relocating
    across the globe, 128–132
    to North America, 125, 126–127
requirements for international nurses,
    129
research
    advocacy and, 159
    degrees, 80–81
    moving to North America, 125
    portfolios, 46–48
    social media and, 140
resources
    curriculum vitae (CV), 8
    degrees, 80–81
    entrepreneurship, 175, 176
    finding programs, 93–95
    government agencies, 129
    mentoring, 122
    portfolios, 55
    resumés, 8
    sharing, 141
responsibilities, mentoring, 105–108
resumés, 3, 4–8, 85
    activities, 16
    automatic tracking systems (ATSs),
        5
    awards, 13, 15–16
    certification/licensure, 10–11
    community service, 18
    cover letters, 21
    cultural impact on, 125
    editing, 8
    education, 12–13
    examples of, 196–199
    experience, 13–15
    expertise, 18–19
    formatting, 9
    goals/objective statements, 9–10
    honors, 13, 15–16
    interviews, 22–29

keywords, 5
portfolios, 32, 35 (*see also* portfolios)
presentations/publications, 16–18
Professional Activities, 12
professional organizations, 16
references, 19
resources, 8
special skills, 18–19
time gaps, 14
volunteer service, 18
writing, 7
reviews
  integrative, 48
  journals, 17
  medical, 170
  narratives, 48
  quality improvement, 170
risks of social media, 137–138
RN to BSN degree program, 72
roles, mentoring, 105–108

S

SBA Small Business Innovative Research (SBIR), 176
schematics, defining nursing identities, 63, 64*f*, 65*f*
scholarships, portfolios, 46
school transcripts, portfolios, 32. *See also* portfolios
searching. *See also* job seeking
  for international nursing jobs, 131, 132–133
  for positions, 3
sections
  of portfolios, 35
  of resumés, 12
self-employment, 184–186. *See also* entrepreneurship
self-reflection, 61–62. *See also* nursing identity
seminars, 37, 38*f*
The 7 Habits of Highly Effective People (Covey), 145

Sigma Theta Tau International (STTI), 81, 158, 176
  Career Center, 8, 96, 111, 124
  joining, 119
  mentorship programs, 110 (*see also* mentoring)
skills
  hard, 6
  interviews, 22–29
  marketing, 184
  nursing, 15
  resumés, 18–19
Skype, 22
sleep routines, 191
Small Business Technology Transfer (SBTT), 176
SMART goals, 114
social media, 135
  benefits of, 137, 139–141
  connecting, 118
  crowd surfing, 149
  expanding networks, 150
  finding mentors, 113, 120
  identifying brands, 141–148 (*see also* branding)
  improving, 148–151
  leveraging, 136–137
  risks of, 137–138
  selecting platforms, 148
South African Nursing Council, 129
speaking English, 130
special skills, resumés, 18–19
spreadsheets, continuing professional development, 38*f*
state licenses, 39. *See also* licenses
statements
  mission, 146–147
  objective, 9–10
  reflective, 53–54
  summary, 53–54
  vision, 145, 146
strategies, work-life balance, 191–194
studies, 46. *See also* research
studying abroad, 132
submitting documents, 4, 84–86
subsections (resumés), formatting, 13

summary statements, 53–54
surveys, 143, 144

T

taxes, filing, 179, 180
technology
    attending conferences, 96
    interviews and, 22
terminal degrees, 72, 76–80
time gaps (resumés), 14
tracking
    continuing professional
        development, 38*f*
    curriculum vitae (CV), 6
    resumés, 5
transcripts, portfolios, 32
translating, 173
Twitter, 159. *See also* social media

U

United States
    post-doctoral fellowships, 127–128
    relocating to, 125, 126–127
USAJOBS, 131
U.S. Bureau of Labor Statistics, 176
U.S. News & World Report, 81
U.S. Nursing Licensure for
    Internationally Educated Nurses,
    127
U.S. Small Business Association, 176

V

values
    core, 142, 143*t*
    identifying, 144
vetting journals, 17
VIA Institute on Character, 143, 144
videoconferencing tools, 178
virtual conferences, 96
virtual interviews, 22
vision statements, 145, 146

visual mind-mapping. *See* mind-
    mapping
voice, using your, 153, 154
    advocacy, 158–160
    dissemination, 155–158
    importance of, 154–155
    networking, 162–164
    political advocacy, 161–162
    professional organizations, 160
volunteer service, 18, 133

W–X–Y

websites, career-building, 8
web sites, designing, 184
wellness coaching, 171
Woodhull Study (STTI), 158, 159
work experience. *See* experience
work-life balance, 187, 188
    current environment of, 190
    dilemma of, 188–189
    imbalance of, 189–190
    strategies, 191–194
workloads, entrepreneurship, 181–
    182
World Health Organization (WHO),
    138
writing
    cover letters, 21
    curriculum vitae (CV), 7, 19–21
    dissemination, 155–158 (*see also*
        voice)
    keywords, 5
    medical writing, 172, 173
    resumés, 3, 7, 9 (*see also* resumés)
    vetting journals, 17 (*see also*
        publications)
    vision statements, 145
WSJ Business, 176

Z

Zoom, 22